COMPLETE POEMS

The Other Voice in Early Modern Europe: The Toronto Series, 34

The Other Voice in
Early Modern Europe:
The Toronto Series

SERIES EDITORS Margaret L. King *and* Albert Rabil, Jr.
SERIES EDITOR, ENGLISH TEXTS Elizabeth H. Hageman

Previous Publications in the Series

MADRE MARÍA ROSA
Journey of Five Capuchin Nuns
Edited and translated by Sarah E. Owens
Volume 1, 2009

GIOVAN BATTISTA ANDREINI
Love in the Mirror: A Bilingual Edition
Edited and translated by Jon R. Snyder
Volume 2, 2009

RAYMOND DE SABANAC AND SIMONE ZANACCHI
Two Women of the Great Schism: The Revelations *of Constance de Rabastens by Raymond de Sabanac and* Life of the Blessed Ursulina of Parma *by Simone Zanacchi*
Edited and translated by Renate Blumenfeld-Kosinski and Bruce L. Venarde
Volume 3, 2010

OLIVA SABUCO DE NANTES BARRERA
The True Medicine
Edited and translated by Gianna Pomata
Volume 4, 2010

LOUISE-GENEVIÈVE GILLOT DE SAINCTONGE
Dramatizing Dido, Circe, and Griselda
Edited and translated by Janet Levarie Smarr
Volume 5, 2010

PERNETTE DU GUILLET
Complete Poems: A Bilingual Edition
Edited by Karen Simroth James
Translated by Marta Rijn Finch
Volume 6, 2010

ANTONIA PULCI
Saints' Lives and Bible Stories for the Stage: A Bilingual Edition
Edited by Elissa B. Weaver
Translated by James Wyatt Cook
Volume 7, 2010

VALERIA MIANI
Celinda, A Tragedy: A Bilingual Edition
Edited by Valeria Finucci
Translated by Julia Kisacky
Annotated by Valeria Finucci and Julia Kisacky
Volume 8, 2010

Enchanted Eloquence: Fairy Tales by Seventeenth-Century French Women Writers
Edited and translated by Lewis C. Seifert and Domna C. Stanton
Volume 9, 2010

GOTTFRIED WILHELM LEIBNIZ, SOPHIE, ELECTRESS OF HANOVER AND QUEEN SOPHIE CHARLOTTE OF PRUSSIA
Leibniz and the Two Sophies: The Philosophical Correspondence
Edited and translated by Lloyd Strickland
Volume 10, 2011

The Other Voice in Early Modern Europe: The Toronto Series

SERIES EDITORS Margaret L. King *and* Albert Rabil, Jr.
SERIES EDITOR, ENGLISH TEXTS Elizabeth H. Hageman

Previous Publications in the Series

In Dialogue with the Other Voice in Sixteenth-Century Italy: Literary and Social Contexts for Women's Writing
Edited by Julie D. Campbell and Maria Galli Stampino
Volume 11, 2011

Sister Giustina Niccolini
The Chronicle of Le Murate
Edited and translated by Saundra Weddle
Volume 12, 2011

Liubov Krichevskaya
No Good without Reward: Selected Writings: A Bilingual Edition
Edited and translated by Brian James Baer
Volume 13, 2011

Elizabeth Cooke Hoby Russell
The Writings of an English Sappho
Edited by Patricia Phillippy
With translations by Jaime Goodrich
Volume 14, 2011

Lucrezia Marinella
Exhortations to Women and to Others if They Please
Edited and translated by Laura Benedetti
Volume 15, 2012

Margherita Datini
Letters to Francesco Datini
Translated by Carolyn James and Antonio Pagliaro
Volume 16, 2012

Delarivier Manley and Mary Pix
English Women Staging Islam, 1696–1707
Edited and introduced by Bernadette Andrea
Volume 17, 2012

Cecilia Del Nacimiento
Journeys of a Mystic Soul in Poetry and Prose
Introduction and prose translations by Kevin Donnelly
Poetry translations by Sandra Sider
Volume 18, 2012

Lady Margaret Douglas and Others
The Devonshire Manuscript: A Women's Book of Courtly Poetry
Edited and introduced by Elizabeth Heale
Volume 19, 2012

Arcangela Tarabotti
Letters Familiar and Formal
Edited and translated by Meredith K. Ray and Lynn Lara Westwater
Volume 20, 2012

The Other Voice in Early Modern Europe: The Toronto Series

SERIES EDITORS Margaret L. King *and* Albert Rabil, Jr.
SERIES EDITOR, ENGLISH TEXTS Elizabeth H. Hageman

Previous Publications in the Series

PERE TORRELLAS AND JUAN DE FLORES
Three Spanish Querelle *Texts:* Grisel and Mirabella, The Slander against Women, *and* The Defense of Ladies against Slanderers*: A Bilingual Edition and Study*
Edited and translated by Emily C. Francomano
Volume 21, 2013

BARBARA TORELLI BENEDETTI
Partenia, a Pastoral Play: A Bilingual Edition
Edited and translated by Lisa Sampson and Barbara Burgess-Van Aken
Volume 22, 2013

FRANÇOIS ROUSSET, JEAN LIEBAULT, JACQUES GUILLEMEAU, JACQUES DUVAL AND LOUIS DE SERRES
Pregnancy and Birth in Early Modern France: Treatises by Caring Physicians and Surgeons (1581–1625)
Edited and translated by Valerie Worth-Stylianou
Volume 23, 2013

MARY ASTELL
The Christian Religion, as Professed by a Daughter of the Church of England
Edited by Jacqueline Broad
Volume 24, 2013

SOPHIA OF HANOVER
Memoirs (1630–1680)
Edited and translated by Sean Ward
Volume 25, 2013

KATHERINE AUSTEN
Book M: A London Widow's Life Writings
Edited by Pamela S. Hammons
Volume 26, 2013

ANNE KILLIGREW
"My Rare Wit Killing Sin": Poems of a Restoration Courtier
Edited by Margaret J. M. Ezell
Volume 27, 2013

TULLIA D'ARAGONA AND OTHERS
The Poems and Letters of Tullia d'Aragona and Others: A Bilingual Edition
Edited and translated by Julia L. Hairston
Volume 28, 2014

LUISA DE CARVAJAL Y MENDOZA
The Life and Writings of Luisa de Carvajal y Mendoza
Edited and translated by Anne J. Cruz
Volume 29, 2014

Russian Women Poets of the Eighteenth and Early Nineteenth Centuries: A Bilingual Edition
Edited and translated by Amanda Ewington
Volume 30, 2014

The Other Voice in
Early Modern Europe:
The Toronto Series

Previous Publications in the Series

JACQUES DU BOSC
L'Honnête Femme: The Respectable Woman in Society *and the* New Collection of Letters and Responses by Contemporary Women
Edited and translated by Sharon Diane Nell and Aurora Wolfgang
Volume 31, 2014

LADY HESTER PULTER
Poems, Emblems, and *The Unfortunate Florinda*
Edited by Alice Eardley
Volume 32, 2014

JEANNE FLORE
Tales and Trials of Love, Concerning Venus's Punishment of Those Who Scorn True Love and Denounce Cupid's Sovereignity: A Bilingual Edition and Study
Edited and translated by Kelly Digby Peebles
Poems translated by Marta Rijn Finch
Volume 33, 2014

VERONICA GAMBARA

Complete Poems

A BILINGUAL EDITION

Critical introduction by

MOLLY M. MARTIN

Edited and translated by

MOLLY M. MARTIN AND PAOLA UGOLINI

ITER

Iter Inc.
Centre for Reformation and Renaissance Studies
Toronto
2014

Iter: Gateway to the Middle Ages and Renaissance
Tel: 416/978-7074 Email: iter@utoronto.ca
Fax: 416/978-1668 Web: www.itergateway.org

Centre for Reformation and Renaissance Studies
Victoria University in the University of Toronto
Tel: 416/585-4465 Email: crrs.publications@utoronto.ca
Fax: 416/585-4430 Web: www.crrs.ca

Printed in Canada.

Iter and the Centre for Reformation and Renaissance Studies gratefully acknowledge the generous support of James E. Rabil, in memory of Scottie W. Rabil, toward the publication of this book.

Library and Archives Canada Cataloguing in Publication
Gàmbara, Veronica, 1485-1550
[Poems]
Complete poems / Veronica Gambara ; critical introduction by Molly M. Martin ; edited and translated by Molly M. Martin and Paola Ugolini. — A bilingual edition.

(The other voice in early modern Europe : The Toronto series ; 34)
Includes bibliographical references and index.
Issued in print and electronic formats.

Poems in Italian with English translations; remaining text in English.
ISBN 978-0-7727-2168-6 (pbk.)
ISBN 978-0-7727-2169-3 (pdf)

1. Gàmbara, Veronica, 1485–1550—Translations into English. 2. Gàmbara, Veronica, 1485–1550—Criticism and interpretation. I. Ugolini, Paola, editor, translator II. Martin, Molly M., editor, translator, writer of added commentary III. Victoria University (Toronto, Ont.). Centre for Reformation and Renaissance Studies, issuing body IV. Iter Inc, issuing body V. Title. VI. Series: Other voice in early modern Europe. Toronto series ; 34

PQ4623.G2A2 2014 851'.3 C2014-902751-6
C2014-902752-4

Cover illustration: Correggio (Antonio Allegri). Portrait of a Lady. Oil on canvas. 103x87.5 cm. Italy. Circa 1518. Inv. no. GE-5555. The State Hermitage Museum, St. Petersburg. Photograph © The State Hermitage Museum / photo by Vladimir Terebenin, Leonard Kheifets, Yuri Molodkovets.

Cover design:
Maureen Morin, Information Technology Services, University of Toronto Libraries.

Typesetting and production:
Iter Inc.

For our parents

Contents

Acknowledgments

Many people have helped bring this book into being through their guidance and generosity. This book would not have been possible were it not for the steadfast support of our editor, Al Rabil Jr., who first recommended that Veronica Gambara join the chorus of women's voices represented in the Other Voice series. We especially appreciate his unwavering patience throughout the years of the manuscript's development as he masterfully guided our work to its completion.

Our most heartfelt thanks go to Virginia Cox, who not only introduced us to the poetry of Veronica Gambara, but also introduced us to each other in suggesting that we collaborate on this translation. She gave invaluable feedback on countless drafts of poems, and she was exceedingly generous with her expertise in sharing her own original scholarship and translations. She was a constant source of guidance and inspiration, which she remains today.

We are grateful to Jane Tylus, who also supported the project by reading multiple drafts of poems and offering insights that always helped us improve the quality of our work.

The anonymous readers on the board of the Centre for Reformation and Renaissance Studies at Victoria University in the University of Toronto offered helpful comments on the manuscript, and Maura High and Lindsay Eufusia gave acute attention to detail in the crucial stages of editing and proofing the manuscript; we thank them all.

To our colleagues at Columbia University, New York University, and the University at Buffalo (SUNY), we thank you for your continued support and friendship.

Introduction

The Other Voice

"The voice [...] that honors Brescia"
—Pietro Bembo

Veronica Gambara (1485–1550) was one of the earliest women writers of lyric poetry known throughout Italy in the first half of the sixteenth century. Through her ancestors in the Nogarola family of Verona and the Pio of Carpi, Gambara shared a unique connection to the learned women of the humanistic milieu in the fifteenth century.[1] This lineage

1. On the women of the Nogarola family and on women humanists of fifteenth-century Italy more broadly, see Phyllis R. Brown, Laurie J. Churchill, and Jane E. Jeffrey, eds., *Women Writing Latin: From Roman Antiquity to Early Modern Europe*, vol. 3, *Early Modern Women Writing Latin* (New York: Routledge, 2002); Silvia R. Fiore, "The Silent Scholars of Italian Humanism: Feminism in the Renaissance," in *Interpreting the Italian Renaissance: Literary Perspectives*, ed. Antonio Toscano (Stony Brook, NY: Forum Italicum, 1991), 15–27; Lisa Jardine, "Women and Humanists: An Education for What?," in *Feminism & Renaissance Studies*, ed. Lorna Hutson (Oxford: Oxford University Press, 1999), 48–81; Margaret L. King and Albert Rabil Jr., eds., *Her Immaculate Hand: Selected Works by and about the Women Humanists of Quattrocento Italy* (Asheville, NC: Pegasus Press, 1997); Margaret L. King, "Thwarted Ambitions: Six Learned Women of the Italian Renaissance," *Soundings* 59 (1976): 267–304; Margaret L. King, "The Religious Retreat of Isotta Nogarola (1418–1466): Sexism and Its Consequences in the Fifteenth Century," *Signs* 3 (1978): 807–22; Margaret L. King, "Book-Lined Cells: Women and Humanism in the Early Italian Renaissance," in *Beyond Their Sex: Learned Women of the European Past*, ed. Patricia H. Labalme (New York: New York University Press, 1980), 66–90; Margaret L. King, *Women of the Renaissance* (Chicago: Chicago University Press, 1991); Holt Parker, "Latin and Greek Poetry by Five Renaissance Italian Women Humanists," in *Sex and Gender in Medieval and Renaissance Texts: The Latin Tradition*, ed. Barbara K. Gold, Paul Allen Miller, and Charles Platter (Albany: State University of New York Press, 1997), 247–85; Jane Stevenson, "Women and Classical Education in the Early Modern Period," in *Women's Education in Early Modern Europe: A History, 1500–1800*, ed. Barbara J. Whitehead (New York: Garland Publications, 1999), 83–109; Jane Stevenson, "Female Authority and Authorization Strategies in Early Modern Europe," in *This Double Voice: Gendered Writing in Early Modern England*, ed. Danielle Clarke and Elizabeth Clarke (Basingstoke, UK: Macmillan, 2000), 16–40; Jane Stevenson, *Women Latin Poets: Language, Gender, and Authority from Antiquity to the Eighteenth Century* (Oxford: Oxford University Press, 2005).

may well have influenced Gambara's early literary aspirations, but it also provided a pedigree that reinforced her legitimacy as an intellect in her own right. At the turn of the century, with the rise of the vernacular as the poetic language of choice and the emergence of the *poesia cortigiana* tradition among the signorial circles of Gambara's northern Italian surroundings, she joined the literary chorus as a young woman with her own lyric love poetry in the vernacular.[2] Gambara wrote primarily in the Italian sonnet form, but she also composed verse in forms suited for musical adaptation, such as the madrigal and *frottola-barzelletta*. Gambara was in fact the first woman in the Italian tradition to publish secular vernacular lyrics, when her madrigal "Or passata è la speranza" (Now hope has gone) was published in 1505 in a collection of musical ballads.[3] As far as we are able to date Gambara's extant poetry, there appears to be a hiatus in the circulation and perhaps in the production of her verse beginning around 1519 and lasting until 1529. This break is most likely attributable to the sudden death in 1518 of Gambara's husband, Giberto X of Correggio, while serving in battle as a military *condottiere*. Under the stipulations of Giberto's will, Gambara was designated guardian of their two young sons and appointed to manage her husband's estate as the regent dowager of Correggio—a role she fulfilled until her death in 1550.[4]

Gambara maintained a welcome and celebrated presence on the literary landscape in both stages of her poetic career. Pietro Bembo (1470–1547) was the first notable member of the literary community to honor Gambara's literary talents. In 1504, he and Gambara exchanged original poems; his identification of Gambara as "la voce [...] che Brescia onora" (the voice [...] that honors Brescia) in the final line of a sonnet indicates that Gambara had acquired a degree of regional fame as a young lyrical poet at the time of the composition.[5]

2. Virginia Cox, *Women's Writing in Italy: 1400–1650* (Baltimore: Johns Hopkins University Press, 2008), 50–53.

3. See Allan Bullock's catalogue of Gambara's presence in various publications, in Veronica Gambara, *Le Rime*, ed. Alan Bullock (Florence: Olschki; Perth: University of Western Australia Press, 1995), 36; Cox, *Women's Writing in Italy*, 51.

4. Baldassare Camillo Zamboni, "Vita di Veronica Gambara," in *Rime e lettere di Veronica Gambara*, ed. Felice Rizzardi (Brescia: Giammaria Rizzardi, 1759), 44.

5. The title of Bembo's sonnet to Gambara is "Certo ben mi poss'io dir pago omai."

Later in the century, Bembo included his early literary exchange with Gambara in the appendix of the 1535 edition of his *Rime*. Ludovico Ariosto (1474–1533) also made early note of Gambara's presence in court circles in the 1516 edition of his *Orlando furioso*, where he names her among the honorable ladies of Correggio. He repeats the honor by underscoring Gambara's literary talent in canto 46 of his final 1532 edition, where she is said to please the poetic muses: "sì grata a Febo e al santo aonio coro" (so dear to Phoebus, and to the sacred Aonian chorus).[6] In canto 37 of Ariosto's epic poem there is a longer celebration of another female poet who had acquired acclaim throughout Italy at the time: the Marchioness of Pescara, Vittoria Colonna (1490–1547). Colonna's poetry was included alongside Gambara's in Bembo's 1535 *Rime* index.[7] As recent scholars have argued, the responsiveness of Bembo and Ariosto to the poetry of Gambara, and their even more enthusiastic reception of Colonna, in the third decade of the sixteenth century, attest to the male literary world's openness, if not eagerness, to engage with women writers.[8]

Throughout the first decades of the sixteenth century, the lives of Gambara and Colonna were strikingly similar. Both women were highly educated members of the upper echelons of Italian society, connected by birth and marriage to prominent ruling families—though Colonna was of higher noble standing and greater political stature

6. Ludovico Ariosto, *Orlando furioso* (Milan: Mondadori editore, 1976), 1207.

7. Cox, *Women's Writing in Italy*, 60.

8. For the emergence of the female writer on the early modern Italian landscape, see Abigail Brundin's introduction to Vittoria Colonna, *Sonnets for Michelangelo, a Bilingual Edition*, ed. and trans. Abigail Brundin (Chicago: University of Chicago Press, 2005); Virginia Cox, "Women Writers and the Canon in Sixteenth-Century Italy: The Case of Vittoria Colonna," in *Strong Voices, Weak History: Early Modern Women Writers and Canons in England, France, and Italy*, ed. Pamela Joseph Benson and Victoria Kirkham (Ann Arbor: University of Michigan Press, 2005), 14–31; Cox, *Women's Writing in Italy*; Carlo Dionisotti, "Appunti sul Bembo e su Vittoria Colonna," in *Miscellanea Augusto Campana*, ed. Rino Avesani et al. (Padua: Antenore, 1981), 257–86; Fabio Finotti, "Women Writers in Renaissance Italy: Courtly Origins of New Literary Canons," in Benson and Kirkham, *Strong Voices, Weak History*, 121–45; Giovanna Rabitti, "Vittoria Colonna, Bembo e Firenze: Un caso di recezione e qualche postilla," *Studi e problemi di critica testuale* 44 (1992): 127–55; Nadia Cannata Salamone, "Women and the Making of the Italian Literary Canon," in *Women in Italian Renaissance Culture and Society*, ed. Letizia Panizza (London: Legenda Press, 2000), 498–512.

by virtue of her baronial rank and her family lineage, which linked her to the powerful Montefeltro dynasty. Gambara and Colonna each married prominent military generals, both of whom died in battle in the first quarter of the century, and both Gambara and Colonna remained widows for the remainder of their lives.[9] Both women proved to be exceedingly talented composers of lyrical vernacular verse in the Bembist *petrarchismo* tradition, and although Colonna's poetic star ultimately outshone that of Gambara, the synchronous rise to fame of the two poets established a tradition, whereby they remained closely linked.[10]

A fascinating point of divergence, however, may be found in the thematic preoccupations of the two female lyricists. Colonna's verse crafts a literary identity centered on her widowhood, beginning with the expression in the *Rime amorose* (Love poems) of a devout widow grieving the loss of the virtuous conjugal love shared with her husband. This thematic of the chaste and grieving widow evolved, with some overlap and key variations, into Colonna's *Rime spirituali* (Spiritual poems), where devotion to the virtuous beloved shifts into a profoundly Christianized spiritual meditation. In contrast, in Gambara's extant poetry, only three poems might speak of grief in widowhood; on her return to the literary scene in 1529, hers is a poetic voice deeply immersed in the occasions of the public and distinctly political spheres. In fact, Gambara announces this thematic shift in a sonnet composed for Colonna in 1532, "Mentre da vaghi e giovenil penseri" (While [I was nourished] by wandering and youthful thoughts): repenting the love-driven wanderings of her early poetic career, she jettisons her "già care rime" (once-dear rhymes) and lets them sink into "silenzo eterno" (eternal silence).[11]

Gambara's role as the dowager Countess of Correggio deeply influenced the second half of her life, including the content and even the

9. Colonna's husband, Ferrante d'Avalos, died in battle in 1525.

10. A poem by Lucia Bertani dell'Oro (1521–67) named Gambara and Colonna the "Sappho and Corinna" of their age. The pairing of Gambara and Colonna also occurs in contemporary analysis, as when Virginia Cox identifies the poets as the "founding mothers" of women's writing in the first half of the sixteenth century. Cox, *Women's Writing in Italy*, 76.

11. Colonna's sonnet in reply, "Lasciar non posso i miei saldi pensieri," affirms her commitment to the theme of love in her verse in honor of the memory of her virtuous husband.

style of the poetry she produced throughout this period. Whereas her early verse concentrates on the internal workings of the poet-persona's dramatic self, tracing the emotional fluctuations of the private mind following the Petrarchan love-lyric model, Gambara's mature work harmonizes with the occasions of the public domain; the poet's subject is no longer the internal self but the external world around her. In these poems, Gambara tells of her surroundings, of the significant political proceedings of her day, and, most pointedly, of the central cultural and political figures responsible for bringing these events into being.

The history of Italian letters from the fourteenth century onward is replete with women who drew on their literary talents to engage in the public sphere. Among the examples of the nexus of women, literature, and politics in Italy during this period is the correspondence between fourteenth-century women humanists and their learned male counterparts, and the Latin orations of the women of the Montefeltro, Visconti, and Sforza dynasties.[12] Gambara dovetails with this well-established tradition in that she worked innovatively with lyric poetry to participate in the political discourses of her time; indeed, Gambara's mature verse provides one of the first examples of a female voice following political events through the vernacular sonnet form. We may thus align Gambara's literary legacy with the poet-ruler model traditionally practiced by men in power—Lorenzo de' Medici (1449–92), for example—and consider her one of the first women of the Italian tradition to utilize her poetic talent as an instrument of rule.

Veronica Gambara: A Brief Biography

Born in Prato Alboino on November 30, 1485, Veronica Gambara spent her youth on the small feudal estate of her noble family in the Brescia region of northern Italy. Throughout the fifteenth century, Brescia cultivated a distinct presence as a center of erudite learning with which many well-known women humanists, such as Laura Cereta (1469–99) and Cassandra Fedele (1465?–1558), came to be associated.[13] Through geography and ancestry, the Gambara family shared an

12. See King and Rabil, *Her Immaculate Hand.*

13. Stephen D. Bowd, *Venice's Most Loyal City: Civic Identity in Renaissance Brescia* (Cambridge, MA: Harvard University Press, 2010), 36.

intimate connection to the educated women of the humanist movement: Gambara's paternal great-grandmother was Ginevra Nogarola (1417–61/68), the learned writer and sister of the even better-known Isotta Nogarola (1418–66) of Verona.

At her family's court, Gambara began to write poetry while she underwent a classic *studia humanitatis* education.[14] Cultural shifts in the literary landscape played a significant role in Gambara's development as an intellectual and as a poet. At the time that the *lirica cortigiana* tradition was taking shape, the vernacular came to replace Latin as the language of poetry. The lyric poetry produced by women in this period was heavily influenced by the poetic model provided by Petrarch in the *Rerum vulgarium fragmenta*. The Petrarchan model reintroduced poetic meditations on secular themes in conjunction with spiritual verse, which had long been part of the literary landscape. Court women, in particular, were regarded as the principal public for vernacular writings, and they came to expand their role as audience and as producers of refined court entertainment.[15] In close proximity to Gambara, one finds the first women to appear in manuscript culture with poetry in the *lirica cortigiana* mode, Camilla Scarampa (1476–1520) among them, whose poetry was circulating throughout the Brescia region, and Veronica's sister Isotta, whose vernacular poetry had attracted public praise.[16]

Throughout her young adulthood, Gambara exhibited both literary talent and an aspiration to circulate her verse to the public, which she did by making effective use of her family network to reach out to prominent cultural figures such as Isabella d'Este (1474–1539).[17]

14. Stevenson, *Women Latin Poets*, 168.

15. Two examples that illuminate how the developing lyric culture began to be oriented toward women may be found in the Sforza court of Milan: an elaborate pictorial interpretation of Petrarch's *Canzoniere* was produced for Beatrice d'Este (1475–97); also for Beatrice, Gasparo Visconti dedicated a Petrarchan-themed collection of lyrics. To Isabella d'Este, the historian Vincenzo Calmeta offered a commentary on Petrarch's *Canzoniere*. See Cox, *Women's Writing in Italy*, 2–17; Finotti, "Women Writers in Renaissance Italy," 123; Salamone, "Women and the Making of the Italian Literary Canon"; Stevenson, *Women Latin Poets*, 282.

16. Cox, *Women's Writing in Italy*, 50–53.

17. On Gambara's paternal side, Galasso Gambara married Margherita d'Este and Niccolò Gambara married Lucrezia Francesco Gonzaga. On her maternal side, Gambara's cousin

As early as 1503, Gambara's madrigal "Or passata è la speranza" (Now hope has gone) was known to Isabella d'Este.[18] Gambara's literary exchanges with Pietro Bembo during this period, rooted in Bembo's acquaintance with the Gambara family, are another example of her use of an extensive network of family and literary connections. Bembo's father served in the Venetian military alongside her father, Count Giovanni Francesco Gambara (d. 1511), and Bembo corresponded with Gambara's brothers. While Bembo's reputation as a literary authority reached its apex later, on the publication of his *Prose della volgar lingua* (1525), he was already well known earlier in the century for his edition of Petrarch's vernacular works, including an edition of the *Rerum vulgarium fragmenta* with commentary. Gambara addressed Bembo in her sonnet "Non t'ammirar, s'a te, non visto mai" (Do not be surprised if, though I have never seen you), to which he replied favorably with a letter and sonnet of his own in honor of Gambara's poetic talents.

Although the feudal territory of the Gambara family maintained a certain level of independence from Brescia proper, throughout Gambara's lifetime the estate was directly affected by the conflict between Venice and France over the region. During the period of Venetian control of Brescia, Gambara's father, Giovanni Francesco Gambara, served as a *condottiere* for the Venetian forces in the successful defeat of the French army's invasion of northern Italy from 1494 to 1498. When hostilities resumed in 1509, France defeated Venice and the Gambara estate fell under French dominion.[19] The Gambara fiefdom emerged as a powerful supporter of the French, and though it grew in power during the occupation (1509–16), it nevertheless remained vulnerable to forces opposed to the French. Such a conflict

---

Giberto Pio married Elisabetta d'Este.

18. William F. Prizer, "Isabella d'Este and Lucrezia Borgia as Patrons of Music: The Frottola at Mantua and Ferrara," *Journal of the American Musicological Society* 38, no. 1 (1985): 1–33; Claudio Vela, "Poesia in musica: Rime della Gambara e di altri poeti settentrionali in tradizione musicale," in *Veronica Gambara e la poesia del suo tempo nell'Italia settentrionale*, ed. Cesare Bozzetti, Pietro Gibellini, and Ennio Sandal (Florence: Olschki, 1989), 400.

19. For an account of Giovanni Francesco's flight from the battle of Agnadello and his escape to his family's palace in Brescia, where he surrendered control to the French, see Carlo Dionisotti, "Elia Capriolo e Veronica Gambara," in Bozzetti, Gibellini, and Sandal, *Veronica Gambara e la poesia del suo tempo nell'Italia settentrionale*, 16–17.

occurred in 1512, one year after Giovanni Francesco's death, when Gambara's mother, Alda Pio, witnessed the Venetian siege of Brescia as Venice attempted to reoccupy the territory.[20] Because the Gambaras were allied with the French, the Brescian Council of Ten exiled the family from the region in 1516 when Venice resumed control of the territory. It was not until 1529, under the protection of Charles V, that the family returned to power in the region.

Gambara's marriage to Giberto X of Correggio in 1509 provided a propitious consolidation of small fortunes and political alliances for both the families. Her noble ancestry, her humanistic erudition, and her literary talent made her well suited for the Correggio court. A small fiefdom in the Po River valley, Correggio was presided over by lords and military generals who maintained long-standing alliances with the princely powers of northern Italy—particularly the Este and Gonzaga, to whom the Correggio were ancestrally tied.[21] Giberto X, related to Gambara's maternal Pio family through his mother Agnese Pio, was left a widower upon the early death of his first wife, Violante Pico, niece of the reputed *letterato* Giovanni Pico della Mirandola (1463–94). The Correggio family already had some literary standing through the works of Niccolò "Postumo" da Correggio (1450–1508), a *condottiere* for the courts of the d'Este dynasty and a poet renowned for a range of vernacular writings, including theatrical dramas, for court entertainment.[22]

Before Gambara's arrival, the cultural projects of the women of the Correggio family had effectively advanced the public repute of this small seat of power.[23] Agnese Pio (d. 1474) collaborated with her husband, Manfredo da Correggio, to commission the construction of the

20. Bowd, *Venice's Most Loyal City*, 206.

21. Alberto Ghidini, "La contea di Correggio ai tempi di Veronica Gambara," in Bozzetti, Gibellini, and Sandal, *Veronica Gambara e la poesia del suo tempo nell'Italia settentrionale*, 79–80.

22. Niccolò da Correggio, *Opere*, ed. Antonia Tissoni Benvenuti (Bari: Laterza, 1969).

23. For excellent studies on the patronage practices of the Correggio women, see Katherine McIver, "The 'Ladies of Correggio': Veronica Gambara and Her Matriarchal Heritage," *Explorations in Renaissance Culture* 26, no. 1 (2000): 25–44; Katherine McIver, "Two Emilian Noblewomen and Patronage Networks in the Cinquecento," in *Beyond Isabella: Secular Women Patrons of Art in Renaissance Italy*, ed. Sheryl E. Reiss and David G. Wilkins (Kirksville, MO: Truman State University Press, 2001), 159–76; Katherine McIver, *Women,*

San Francesco church, where Manfredo was later buried.[24] In 1475, Cassandra Colleoni, wife of Niccolò da Correggio, expanded the San Francesco structure with the construction of her own family chapel, the Cappella Colleoni. Correggio's Corpo del Cristo church benefited from the patronage of Francesca da Brandenburg (d. 1512), wife of Borso da Correggio (d. 1504); she commissioned a chapel dedicated to the Virgin Mary to serve as the site for her husband's tomb. As a widow, Francesca da Brandenburg dedicated her dowry to the construction of the Palazzo dei Principi in 1507 to serve as the primary residence of Correggio's leaders.[25] Gambara appears to have adapted with ease to the cultural environment. She inherited funds from Francesca to continue her decoration of the church of San Domenico, and she designated a room within the Palazzo dei Principi to serve as her private *studiolo*.[26] Gambara's patronage of the well-known local artist Antonio Allegri (called Correggio, 1489–1534) began as early as 1517, though the more significant projects they collaborated on took place later in the century.[27]

As consort to a feudal lord, Gambara helped forge Correggio's political relations with the surrounding Este and Gonzaga ducal houses. Gambara named her first son Ippolito (1510–52) after the archbishop of Ferrara, Cardinal Ippolito d'Este (1479–1520), who also performed the child's baptism ceremony, held at the court of Isabella d'Este and Francesco Gonzaga (1466–1519) in Mantua. Upon the birth of her second son, Girolamo (1511–72), the following year, Gambara chose a close political friend of Francesco Gonzaga, Francesco Munario, as godfather.[28] The death of Giberto in 1518 led to Gambara's appointment as the regent dowager of Correggio in the government of her husband's fiefdom. As the single woman ruler over a territory she had acquired by inheritance rather than birth, Gambara held a delicate position of power, which relied on strong alliances for military protection

---

Art, and Architecture in Northern Italy, 1520–1580 (Aldershot, UK: Ashgate Publishing, 2006).

24. McIver, "The 'Ladies of Correggio,'" 30.

25. McIver, *Women, Art, and Architecture in Northern Italy*, 66.

26. Zamboni, "Vita di Veronica Gambara," 109.

27. McIver, *Women, Art, and Architecture in Northern Italy*, 124.

28. Zamboni, "Vita di Veronica Gambara," 40.

and economic stability. When war broke out between the French king Francis I (1494–1547) and Charles V (1500–58), Holy Roman emperor and king of Spain, Gambara managed Correggio's alignment with the victorious Spanish power. In 1520, Charles V affirmed his protection of the Gambara territory under the name of her two sons; a brief letter in Latin from Charles to Gambara, dated 1521, marks the first known correspondence between the emperor and the countess.[29]

Gambara also made use of her own family's political capital to buttress her position. The period around 1530 was crucial for the fortune of the Gambara family, due in part to the prestigious positions achieved by Gambara's brothers, Uberto (1489–1549) and Brunoro (d. 1570s). Brunoro elevated his rank in Charles V's army, while Pope Clement VII (r. 1523–34) made Uberto papal governor of the city of Bologna to oversee the coronation of Charles V as Holy Roman emperor.[30] As Charles V and Clement VII reconstituted key territories of the Italian states, the emperor restored the Gambaras to their original feudal territory after their decade of exile. Moreover, the Gambara brothers were able to insert an article in the peace treaty drawn up between Charles V and the Venetian Republic to ensure protection of the Gambara possessions by imperial forces should they ever fall under threat of Venetian invasion.[31]

The exceptional political and social positioning of the Gambara brothers in the most important city in northern Italy at the time provided Veronica Gambara an ideal setting to advance her two sons, both of whom were then of prime age to enter public office. Gambara's elder son, Ippolito, began to serve in the imperial army of Charles V, while Girolamo served under his uncle Uberto for the duration of his tenure as governor of Bologna. In a letter to her secretary Ludovico Rosso, who received Girolamo upon his arrival in Bologna, Gambara casts Girolamo as a natural extension of herself:

29. The Latin text of the letter is in ibid., 51. For Charles V's protection of Correggio, see Ghindi, "La contea di Correggio ai tempi di Veronica Gambara," 84.

30. Zamboni, "Vita di Veronica Gambara," 53. Charles was Holy Roman emperor from 1519 until his abdication in 1556.

31. Riccardo Finzi, *Umanità di Veronica Gambara (1485–1550): Commemorazione pronunciata a Correggio, nel IV centenario della morte della poetessa, il 28 maggio 1950* (Reggio Emilia: Tipolitografia Emiliana, 1969), 16.

> Il Sig. Girolamo mio figlio viene tanto allegro, quanto si possa dire, e starà appresso di Monsignore; io ve lo raccomando non solamente come figliuolo mio, ma come una parte di me stessa, e che dico io una parte, s'egli è il tutto! Ve lo raccomando adunque come me stessa, poichè egli è la Veronica medesima.
>
> (My son Girolamo is extremely happy to arrive, as much as one can say, and he will be staying with my brother; I pass him on to you not only as my son, but as a part of me, though I say "a part" when I mean he is all of me! I pass him on to you then as myself, in that he is the equal of Veronica.)[32]

Gambara's way of presenting her son illuminates the representative nature of kinship within ruling families, in that the eminence of Gambara's sons, and indeed that of her entire family, was coterminous with her own public reputation in many ways.

Gambara resided in Bologna for a number of months to be in the company of the most illustrious political and cultural figures of the day. During this period, she returned to the public circulation of her poetry by sending the sonnet "A l'ardente desio ch'ognor m'accende" (The burning desire that ever inspires me) to Pietro Bembo in 1529, to which he replied with the sonnet "Quel dolce suon, per cui chiaro s'intende" (That sweet sound, so clear to all who hear). Gambara secured her standing among the community of elite *letterati* through her poetic activity in this second stage of her life, but her poetry also helped her carve out a unique cultural space, whereby she was able to foster not only her cultural reputation but her political prosperity as well. This is most evident in Gambara's use of poetry to sustain her connection to Charles V—a political aim that dominated Gambara's diplomacy from 1530 forward, and which held implications for the careers of her sons, the reputation of her family, and the security of her fiefdom.

Over the course of Charles V's frequent visits to the states of the Po River valley, the courts competed in their artistic projects to

32. Gambara, *Rime e lettere di Veronica Gambara*, ed. Felice Rizzardi, 171.

celebrate the newly crowned emperor.[33] Gambara hosted Charles V at her Correggio court on his journey out of Italy in 1530 after the historic congress in Bologna that established the peace between Francis I and Charles. In preparation, she undertook a major civic development, calling on the artist Correggio to oversee the construction of a street, the Viale dell'Imperatore, for the imperial procession upon his arrival. Gambara also commissioned the artist to decorate the interior of the Palazzo dei Principi with two frescoes, including one of Mary Magdalen in a penitent pose—a discreet reference to the piety and virtue of the countess; the penitent Magdalen was used in a similar way by Italian Renaissance noblewomen across the region.[34] The frescoes were destroyed with the destruction of the palace in 1556.[35] More enduring, however, was the series of sonnets that Gambara composed in honor of Charles V in the third and fourth decades of the century, through which she was able to demonstrate not only her devotion to him but also the steadfast attention with which she followed the politics of empire playing out on an international scale.

Other poems of Gambara's mature oeuvre convey her support of the emperor's political campaigns across Italy, such as his work with Alessandro Farnese (Pope Paul III, r. 1534–49) in the fight of Christendom against the Ottoman Empire, and in more local enterprises, such as the return of the Medici family to the government of Florence, orchestrated by Charles V and Clement VII in 1530. Gambara's support of the Medici restoration is elaborately delineated in a twenty-seven-stanza narrative poem (the *Stanze*) composed in ottava rima, "Quando miro la terra ornata e bella" (When I behold the beautiful land, bountifully adorned), in which she calls for a return to the golden age of Medici rule under the legacy of Lorenzo "il Magnifico."

33. For the cultural enterprises of the northern courts in honor of Charles V, see William Eisler, "The Impact of the Emperor Charles V upon the Italian Visual Culture, 1529–1533," *Arte lombarda* 65 (1983): 93–110; Marcello Fantoni, "Carlo V e l'immagine dell'*imperator*," in *Carlo V e l'Italia*, ed. Marcello Fantoni (Rome: Bulzoni, 2000), 77–101.

34. For the representation of the penitent Magdalen as an icon of virtue for Italian noblewomen, see Susan Haskins, *Mary Magdalen: Myth and Metaphor* (New York: Harcourt, 1993); Marjorie Och, "Vittoria Colonna and the Commission for a *Mary Magdalen* by Titian," in Reiss and Wilkins, *Beyond Isabella*, 193–223.

35. Correggio was sacked by the Spanish army after the abdication of the emperor.

Gambara's literary activity throughout her governing years, in her poetry as well as her correspondence, elucidates the interrelationship between cultural currency and political power so characteristic of Renaissance Italy. But these dual roles did not always strike an equal balance. In some instances, Gambara struggled to connect with viable sources of poetic inspiration. In a letter to Pietro Bembo composed in 1538, Gambara writes:

> Quanto al mandarle qualcuna delle mie composizioni, già le ho scritto che la vena dell'usato ingegno è secca; pure, se le Muse non mi lasceranno in tutto, cercherò di ubbidirla, e solamente per ubbidirla, sapendo quanto le mie roche e basse rime siano indegne di comparire sotto l'altera vista del suo intelletto avezza a mirar luce divina.
>
> (As for sending you some of my works, I have already written you that the vein of my earlier talent is dried out; yet, should the Muses not abandon me altogether, I will seek to obey you, and I will do this solely to obey you, knowing full well how my coarse and lowly rhymes are unworthy to appear to the noble sight of your intellect, used to contemplate divine light.)[36]

A distinct echo of this diffidence may be heard in Gambara's sonnet to Pietro Aretino from the same period, where she again describes the withholding Muses: "Voglion le Muse l'ozio e il tempo aprico; / a me Fortuna è dura più che smalto; / il verno mi combatte, e il mar nemico" (The Muses require leisure and pleasant times; to me Fortune is harder than enamel, the winter battles against me, and the sea is my enemy).

In a sonnet to another prominent figure among literary circles, the prolific Venetian writer Ludovico Dolce (1508–68), Gambara presents herself as a poet of limited ability, describing her talent as "rozzo" and "debile" (coarse and weak) in the first tercet. Certainly this humble posture is a product of Gambara's strict adherence to the

36. Gambara, *Rime e lettere di Veronica Gambara*, ed. Felice Rizzardi, 123–24.

traditional ethos of feminine modesty; yet it must also reflect some sense of how the demands of her life as the governing regent may have encroached upon any idea of exploring a purely poetic vocation. Indeed, throughout these years, Gambara sets out with her pen to advance the public careers of her two sons, to foster relations with and broadcast support for important political allies, and to distill her positions on the significant political events of her time. In a letter written in 1540 to Bembo—who himself integrated cultural and political enterprises throughout his life, especially on his appointment as cardinal under Pope Paul III in 1539—Gambara demonstrates the combined literary, political, and uniquely personal dynamics that developed in their relationship over the years:

> Mi parrebbe commettere grandissimo errore, se venendo il Sig. Jeronimo mio in quelle parti non facessi riverenza a V.S. Reverendiss. con questa mia, poichè con la presenza, siccome desidero, non posso. La supplico adunque che si ricordi, che io sono in questo istante, quella stessa che era già tanti anni, e benchè abbia cangiato il pelo, non ho però cangiato voglia, anzi siccome in lei crescono degnità e valore, in me parimente si raddoppiano amore e servitù.
>
> (I would be afraid of committing a great mistake if, given that my son Girolamo is coming to your area [Rome], I did not impart reverence to Your Excellency with this letter of mine, since I could not do this in person, although I wish I could. I pray you remember that I am in this moment the same person I was many years ago, and though my hair has changed in color, my will remains unchanged; for as much as virtue and dignity have grown in you, so love and reverence increase in me, equally.)[37]

Here again we see the connection between Gambara and the reputation of her son Girolamo, now promoted within the offices of the

37. Ibid.,126.

church and in service in the papal court at the time of Bembo's appointment as cardinal. From 1539 forward, Girolamo worked with the papal legate Cardinal Alessandro Farnese (grandson of Pope Paul III), and in 1546, he played a significant role in arranging the alliance between the papacy and Charles V to combat the threat from France.[38] In Gambara's letter to Bembo, she includes "un mio sonetto non visto da niuno" (a sonnet of mine, not seen by anyone), a politically themed composition in praise of Pope Paul III as the leader of Christendom in the war against the Ottoman Empire.[39] Gambara fosters intimacy with her correspondent by noting her age (the reference to her graying hair) as she simultaneously provides crucial support to multiple key figures in the Italian political realm (Cardinal Pietro Bembo and Pope Alessandro Farnese) in both epistolary and lyric forms.

Like Bembo, Gambara approached Vittoria Colonna as an important figure at the center of an influential cultural and political network. Both poets were writers of lyric poetry on the contemporary literary stage, but the subservient tone in which Gambara addresses Colonna in her verse draws attention to the superiority of Colonna's noble rank and poetic repute. Gambara's second sonnet to Colonna composed in 1532, "O de la nostra etade unica gloria" (Oh sole glory of our age), celebrates her contemporary as an icon of literary talent and virtue. In the sonnet, Gambara calls on members of the female sex to erect a temple in Colonna's honor, though it was Gambara's sonnet that in fact helped fortify Colonna's "monumental" status as the female Apollo of the era. Lodovico Domenichi (1515–64) published the sonnet in his anthology of women's poetry in 1559, which subsequently gave rise to a tradition of imitation of the sonnet in other tribute poems by women lyric poets of the century.[40] Gambara's association with Colonna assuredly added lustre to Gambara's literary reputation; at the same time, Gambara was also motivated to foster a close connection to Colonna because of her relation to the politically prestigious d'Avalos family.

38. Antonia Chimenti, *Veronica Gambara: Gentildonna del rinascimento; Un intreccio di poesia e storia* (Reggio Emilia: Magis Books, 1995), 62.

39. See sonnet 60 in the current edition.

40. Cox, *Women's Writing in Italy*, 69.

The Marquis of Vasto Alfonso d'Avalos (1502–46), the cousin of Colonna's deceased husband Ferrante d'Avalos, served as a prominent general in Charles V's imperial army. A poet himself, d'Avalos visited Gambara's Correggio residence in 1531 in the company of Ariosto, during which Gambara offered Ariosto a small pension to support his writing of the *Orlando furioso*.[41] In 1540, Gambara wrote to d'Avalos asking him to "[t]ener memoria del Sig. Ippolito mio figliuolo, tanto servitore di V. E. quanto ella medesima sa, alla quale bacio le mani, desiderando felice fine a tutti gli altri desideri" (keep a memory of my son Signor Ippolito, a great servant to Your Excellency, as you yourself know, and I kiss your hand wishing for happy fulfillment of all your other desires).[42] Her effort was successful, as Ippolito was elevated to a more prominent role in the general's circle.

From 1543 to 1544, when d'Avalos and Gambara's son Ippolito served together in the battles taking place to the north against the French, Gambara composed three sonnets for the d'Avalos family, depicting Maria d'Aragona's endurance of her husband's absence in war.[43] In addition to her correspondence with the general and to her composition of verse in honor of the couple, Gambara pursued a further enterprise in support of the prominent family: she commissioned the Correggio scholar Rinaldo Corso (1525–82) to compile a collection of Vittoria Colonna's spiritual verse with his own commentary in 1541. Corso's edition was published in 1543; a second, enlarged edition appeared in 1558.[44] Colonna's *Rime spirituali* explore Reformist ideas as they circulated among literary and intellectual circles throughout the 1540s, which drew the interest of Pietro Bembo and Maria

41. Zamboni, "Vita di Veronica Gambara," 67; Ghindi, "La contea di Correggio ai tempi di Veronica Gambara," 93.

42. Gambara, *Rime e lettere di Veronica Gambara*, ed. Felice Rizzardi, 146.

43. See sonnets 43, 44, and 45 in the current edition.

44. Cox, *Women's Writing in Italy*, 67. For a study of the manuscript, see Monica Bianco, "Rinaldo Corso e il 'Canzoniere' di Vittoria Colonna," *Italique: Poésie italienne de la Renaissance* 1 (1998): 35–45. Konrad Eisenbichler provides an extensive discussion of another, much earlier, instance of a published commentary of an early modern woman writer: Alessandro Piccolomini's published commentary of Virginia Salvi's poem in 1541. See chapter 4, "Virginia Martini Salvi: An Indomitable Woman," in *The Sword and the Pen: Women, Politics, and Poetry in Sixteenth-Century Siena* (Ann Arbor: University of Notre Dame Press, 2012).

d'Aragona.[45] It is likely that Gambara encountered these ideas through Colonna's verse in the collection she commissioned from Corso, and one sonnet of her own spiritually themed verse—"Scelse da tutta la futura gente" ([The noble and infinite Goodness] chose from the future people)—appears to reflect this exploration. While Gambara did not retreat to a spiritual seclusion in her widowhood, she did use poetry to mark significant historical moments within the politics of the church, such as the death of Pope Clement VII in 1534 and the congress in Bologna, called by Pope Paul III, to negotiate a peace treaty between Charles V and Francis I.

Gambara surrounded herself with religious iconography consisting of select *exempla* of her Christian virtue in widowhood. I have already mentioned the penitent Magdalen fresco in her Palazzo residence. Two years before her death, in preparation for her eventual burial, Gambara commissioned a painting of Saint Jerome for her chapel project. The Saint Jerome figure emblematized Gambara's devotion to piety and chastity in her widowhood, virtues that Jerome had come to represent through his epistles to widows, which emphasized these qualities in particular.[46] The final years of Gambara's life were spent at Correggio, where she maintained close ties with a variety of correspondents. Gambara died in 1550, at the age of sixty-five, and was buried next to her husband in the church of San Domenico.

45. Introduction to Colonna, *Vittoria Colonna: Sonnets for Michelangelo*, 1–43; Cox, *Women's Writing in Italy*, 73.

46. McIver, *Women, Art, and Architecture in Northern Italy*, 178. On Saint Jerome and widowhood, see Caroline Murphy, *Lavinia Fontana: A Painter and Her Patrons in Sixteenth-Century Bologna* (New Haven, CT: Yale University Press, 2003), especially chapter 5, "'La Vita Vedovile': The Art of Widowhood"; Eugene F. Rice, *Saint Jerome in the Renaissance* (Baltimore: Johns Hopkins University Press, 1985); Mary Vaccaro, "Dutiful Widows: Female Patronage and Two Marian Altarpieces by Parmigianino," in Reiss and Wilkins, *Beyond Isabella*, 177–92; Carolyn Valone, "Roman Matrons as Patrons: Various Views of the Cloistered Wall," in *The Crannied Wall*, ed. Craig A. Monson (Ann Arbor: University of Michigan Press, 1992), 49–72; Carolyn Valone, "Piety and Patronage: Women and the Early Jesuits," in *Creative Women in Medieval and Early Modern Italy*, ed. E. Ann Matter and John Coakley (Philadelphia: University of Pennsylvania Press, 1994), 157–84.

Historical Context: The Ruling Dowager

The ascent of a widow to a seat of political power in the absence of a legitimate male heir was common practice among the courts of northern Italy throughout the fifteenth and sixteenth centuries.[47] Signorial women were prepared for the myriad public responsibilities they were expected to fulfill as women of the court, beginning in their youth through the humanist edification program provided to most court children.[48] This education was deemed especially important for court daughters in preparation for the public, and in some cases, political duties women were called to perform as future consorts to rulers—a role that could include temporarily taking over the political affairs of the court in their husbands' absences, perhaps even governing independently as an appointed regent dowager.[49] The education provided

47. For a study of marriage within the Italian princely courts, see Anthony F. d'Elia, *The Renaissance of Marriage in Fifteenth-Century Italy* (Cambridge, MA: Harvard University Press, 2004). See also Natalie Tomas, *The Medici Women: Gender and Power in Renaissance Florence* (Aldershot, UK: Ashgate Publishing, 2003), especially the chapter "The 'Problem' of a Female Ruler."

48. The best-known document attesting to the importance of a humanist education for dynastic daughters is a letter by the humanist Leonardo Bruni (1369–1446) to Battista Montefeltro Malatesta (1383–1450). Bruni's letter may have regarded Battista's own education, or, depending on the date of the letter, it may address the education of her daughter, Elisabetta Malatesta Varano (1407–49).

49. For scholarship on women's humanistic studies that views this education as ornamental, see Jardine, "Women and Humanists," and King, "Book-Lined Cells." These studies address "learned Renaissance women" as a collective group and do not sufficiently distinguish the historical experience of dynastic women of the *signorial* courts from women of lower social rank. I follow the line of Cecil Clough's research on the women of the Montefeltro/Malatesta ruling dynasty and the tradition of educating women from this family in preparation for rule: Clough, "Daughters and Wives of the Montefeltro: Outstanding Bluestockings of the Quattrocento," *Renaissance Studies* 10, no. 1 (1996): 31–55. For further studies that address the education of women in preparation for rule in the Italian court tradition see Anthony F. d'Elia, "Marriage, Sexual Pleasure, and Learned Brides in the Wedding Orations of Fifteenth-Century Italy," *Renaissance Quarterly* 55, no. 2 (2002): 379–433; d'Elia, *The Renaissance of Marriage in Fifteenth-Century Italy*; Fiore, "The Silent Scholars of Italian Humanism"; Werner L. Gundersheimer, "Women, Learning, and Power: Eleonora of Aragon and the Court of Ferrara," in Labalme, *Beyond Their Sex*, 43–65; Stephen Kolsky, "Bending the Rules: Marriage in Renaissance Collections of Biographies of Famous Women," in *Marriage in Italy, 1300–1650*, ed. Trevor Dean and K. J. P. Lowe (Cambridge: Cambridge University Press,

to Gambara in her youth, in conjunction with the model that her mother, Alda Pio, presented in the management of the family feudatory during her husband's absences and as a widow upon his death, helped prepare Gambara for her adult role as the governing regent countess of Correggio.

In the Po River valley region where Gambara lived as consort to Giberto X, women customarily partook in the management of the area's many small fiefdoms in place of husbands who were frequently absent in military service. To the south of Correggio in Scandiano, Silvia Sanvitale Boiardo (d. 1584) assisted her husband, Giulio Boiardo (d. 1550), in the government of the fiefdom, which served as a vassal of the powerful Este family of Ferrara. Later, Duke Ercole II d'Este (1431–1505) granted Silvia Sanvitale Boiardo approval to rule Scandiano in her own right upon her husband's death.[50] To the west in Fontanellato, Paola Gonzaga-Sanvitale (1504–70s) took an active role alongside her husband, Giangaleazzo Sanvitale (1496–1550), in managing the political issues of their fiefdom and was given dominion over the territory until her eldest son came of age.[51] Consorts to ruling husbands were engaged politically to varying degrees in a form of partnership in statecraft[52] and were prepared to fulfill such roles temporarily, as well as permanently upon their husbands' deaths. The ascent of a widow to occupy a seat of power most frequently occurred when the rightful male heir was absent, too young to rule, or incapacitated. There are also instances of widow regency in which the wife provided the legitimate link to the ruling seat through her patrilineal heritage. In all instances, the transfer of power from the ruling husband to his widow depended on the support and tolerance of the male members of court and the family of the female ruler.[53]

1998), 227–48; Dorothy M. Robathon, "A Fifteenth-Century Bluestocking," *Medievalia et humanistica* 2 (1944): 106–11.

50. McIver, "Two Emilian Noblewomen and Patronage Networks in the Cinquecento," 164–68.

51. McIver, *Women, Art, and Architecture in Northern Italy*, 36.

52. Deanna Shemek, *Ladies Errant: Wayward Women and Social Order in Early Modern Italy* (Durham: Duke University Press, 1998), 127.

53. Tomas, *The Medici Women*, 165.

Women and men in positions of political power were responsible for shaping a public image that would justify their rule and facilitate the public's reception of a woman's power.[54] Italian court rulers endeavored to fashion themselves as highly educated, God-fearing devotees to the state; through artistic patronage of church building and religious works of art, rulers made a public display of their piety.[55] The female ruler who governed as a widow naturally sought to align herself with these qualities in her self-presentation to the public; she benefited even further from displaying the ideal behavior prescribed to widows in the early modern period.

The prescriptive literature addressing the appropriate behavior of widows in the sixteenth century addresses primarily the Italian widow of the upper nobility and the patrician class, rather than widows of dynastic status.[56] As is the case with the body of prescriptive

54. Joyce de Vries, "Casting Her Widowhood: The Contemporary and Posthumous Portraits of Caterina Sforza," in *Widowhood and Visual Culture in Early Modern Europe*, ed. Alison Levy (Aldershot, UK: Ashgate Publishing, 2003), 78; Tomas, *The Medici Women*, 166.

55. Clough, "Daughters and Wives of the Montefeltro," 51. See also d'Elia, "Marriage, Sexual Pleasure, and Learned Brides," 422, where in his study of wedding orations in the fifteenth-century courts, he concludes: "While there were clearly different expectations for men and women in Italian courts, brides and grooms are often praised in surprisingly similar ways."

56. For studies on widowhood in the early modern period, see Rudolph M. Bell, *How to Do It: Guides to Good Living for Renaissance Italians* (Chicago: University of Chicago Press, 1999); Judith M. Bennett and Amy M. Froide, eds., *Singlewomen in the European Past, 1250–1800* (Philadelphia: University of Pennsylvania Press, 1999); Lourens van den Bosch and Jan Bremmer, eds., *Between Poverty and the Pyre: Moments in the History of Widowhood* (London: Routledge, 1995); Kevin Brownlee, "Widowhood, Sexuality, and Gender in Christine de Pizan," *Romanic Review* 86, no. 2 (1995): 339–53; Cindy L. Carlson and Angela Jane Weisl, eds., *Constructions of Widowhood and Virginity in the Middle Ages* (New York: St. Martin's Press, 1999); Sandra Cavallo and Lyndan Warner, eds., *Widowhood in Medieval and Early Modern Europe* (New York: Pearson Education, 1999); Isabelle Chabot, "'La sposa in nero': La ritualizzazione del lutto delle vedove fiorentine (secoli XIV–XV)," *Quaderni Storici* 86 (1994): 421–62; Stanley Chojnacki, *Women and Men in Renaissance Venice: Twelve Essays on Patrician Society* (Baltimore: Johns Hopkins University Press, 2000); Virginia Cox, "The Single Self: Feminist Thought and the Marriage Market in Early Modern Venice," *Renaissance Quarterly* 48, no. 3 (1995): 513–81; Amy Louise Erickson, *Women and Property in Early Modern England* (London: Routledge, 1993); Jack Goody, Joan Thrisk, and E. P. Thompson, eds., *Family and Inheritance in Rural Society in Western Europe, 1200–1800* (Cambridge: Cambridge University Press, 1976); Jack Goody, *The Development of Marriage and Family in Medieval Europe* (Cambridge: Cambridge University Press, 1983); David Herlihy, *Women,*

texts written by men that set out to codify women's behavior in the Italian Renaissance, the distance between the condition recommended for widowhood and the real lives and perceptions of noble widows was indeed incalculable.[57] With this disjuncture in mind, these materials may be used as a constructive source for outlining the social ideologies surrounding widowhood in sixteenth-century Italy. Taken together, the sources describe the ideal behavior of noble widows as entailing the display of piety, charity, and spousal devotion in the form of chastity. These widows ideally, but not necessarily, lived in private retreat or in a convent. By and large, patrician widows were to conduct themselves according to sixteenth-century conventional ideals of feminine behavior, though now in the absence of their husbands, they were advised to transfer what was once their devotion to their spouse to a spiritual devotion to God. Naturally, the situation of the ruling widow, because of the very public nature of her duty to her territory, was distinctly at odds with the ideal of the patrician widow, who was to retreat to the private sphere. Yet when one examines the iconography in the patronage pursuits of a typical widow regent, one finds that the fashioning of these qualities—that is, devotion to the memory of her husband and his ruling legacy, a religious piety often exhibited by

---

Family, and Society in Medieval Europe: Historical Essays (1978–1991) (Providence: Berghahn Books, 1995); Diane Owen Hughes, "From Brideprice to Dowry in Mediterranean Europe," *Journal of Family History* 3 (1978): 263–96; Catherine E. King, *Renaissance Women Patrons: Wives and Widows in Italy, 1300–1550* (Manchester: Manchester University Press, 1998); Joan Larson Klein, *Daughters, Wives, and Widows: Writings by Men about Women and Marriage in England* (Urbana: University of Illinois Press, 1992); Christiane Klapisch-Zuber, *Women, Family, and Ritual in Renaissance Italy* (Chicago: University of Chicago Press, 1985); Thomas Kuehn, *Law, Family, and Women: Toward a Legal Anthropology of Renaissance Italy* (Chicago: University of Chicago Press, 1991); Catherine Lawless, "'A Widow of God?' St. Anne and Representations of Widowhood in Fifteenth-Century Florence," in *Women in Renaissance and Early Modern Europe*, ed. Christine Meek (Dublin: Four Courts Press, 2000), 15–42; Allison Levy, *Widowhood and Visual Culture in Early Modern Europe* (Aldershot, UK: Ashgate Publishing, 2003); McIver, *Women, Art, and Architecture in Northern Italy*; Louise Mirrer, ed., *Upon My Husband's Death: Widows in the Literature and Histories of Late Medieval Europe* (Ann Arbor: University of Michigan Press, 1992); Murphy, *Lavinia Fontana*; Tomas, *The Medici Women*; Richard C. Trexler, *Public Life in Renaissance Florence* (Ithaca, NY: Cornell University Press, 1991); Vaccaro, "Dutiful Widows."

57. See Murphy's work, *Lavinia Fontana*, on the portraits by Lavinia Fontana of aristocratic widows of Bologna.

her patronage activity beginning with the burial project and funerary tomb for the deceased husband, and the public display of her chastity to mitigate the threat of losing the husband's seat of power to an outside family—effectively moderated the potential tensions surrounding her role as a woman ruler occupying a temporary seat of power.

Caterina Sforza (1463–1509), for example, became the regent ruler over Imola and Forlì upon the assassination of her husband, Girolamo Riario, in 1488. Caterina's first act as regent was to orchestrate a triumphal ceremony fused with both political and spiritual meaning: on the feast day of Forlì's patron saint, Saint Mercurialis, Caterina added a triumphal entry into Forlì to exhibit the Riario family's hold on power and to place her role as her husband's legitimate political heir on public display. Moreover, Caterina utilized the day to commemorate the honorable burial of her husband in the church that housed many previous Riario rulers to showcase her grief and devotion to his memory publicly as both a spouse and a ruler.[58] One side of a medal portrait of her by Niccolò Fiorentino presents Caterina in modest dress with a veil to signal her widowhood, and beneath this image an inscription that emphasizes her Riario name ("DE RIARIO")—the key link to her political power—and her birth family's name ("SF," for Sforza). This presentation of Caterina as a chaste Riario widow was produced only in relation to her political status as a widow regent; indeed, in a medal struck at the conclusion of Caterina's regency, her image had changed: her widowhood symbol, her veil, had been removed, and her femininity emphasized by flowing hair, an embellished dress, and ornamental jewelry.[59]

Caterina de' Medici (1519–89) is another illuminating example of a widow regent who creatively fashioned the legitimacy of her regency through a series of select public representations.[60] When Caterina de' Medici became the regent for her ten-year-old son in 1560, she was in a challenging position, not only as a regent of a foreign

58. De Vries, "Casting Her Widowhood," 82–83.

59. Ibid., 87.

60. Gambara wrote to Caterina de' Medici in 1534 regarding Leonora of Correggio, the daughter of Gian Galeazzo Correggio and Ginevra Rangone, who went to France to serve as a lady in waiting in Caterina's court. Gambara, *Rime e lettere di Veronica Gambara*, ed. Felice Rizzardi, 97–99.

country (France) but also in presiding over a court that favored her husband's mistress. She staged legitimacy by showcasing her widowhood, appearing always in black, albeit elaborate, mourning dress, both in person and also in all artistic representations of her, thus forging a permanent link with her husband. She also established a lavish monument to the memory of her husband with whose construction her name would be forever associated. In addition, she aligned herself with the classical figure Artemisia—a widow who mourned the loss of her husband, after whose death she ruled authoritatively in his stead—by commissioning from Antoine Caron a series of tapestry drawings of this iconic figure.[61]

Gambara was keenly aware of the power of self-representation as a means to support her political power. This is most evident in her cultural undertakings throughout her regency, particularly her poetic activity from 1529 onward, as they were primarily charged with the objective of manifesting her virtue, piety, and fitness for rule. Gambara's political position proved a shaping influence on the reemergence of her poetics, not only by facilitating her rise to recognition in the literary landscape, but also in determining her creative choices as a lyricist; the production of poetry served as a key site in the construction of her image as a legitimate widow ruler and as an icon of feminine virtue.

Analysis of Gambara's Writings

> "Base thoughts no longer reside in me."
> —Veronica Gambara

Gambara's love poetry from the first period of her poetic career consists primarily of individual episodic meditations that describe the inner emotional turmoil rooted in the poet-persona's suffering in love. As befits her subject, the Petrarchan sonnet is the dominant lyric

61. For an excellent study of Caterina de' Medici's Artemisia iconography, see Sheila ffolliott, "Catherine de' Medici as Artemisia: Figuring the Powerful Widow," in *Rewriting the Renaissance: The Discourses of Sexual Difference in Early Modern Europe*, ed. Margaret W. Ferguson, Maureen Quilligan, and Nancy J. Vickers (Chicago: University of Chicago Press, 1986), 227–41.

form, though Gambara also experimented successfully with other popular lyric forms, including the madrigal, *frottola-barzelletta*, and *strambotto* in ottava rima. The weight of inevitability in the poet's conveyed desire—time and time again unfulfilled, and yet ultimately everlasting—is tempered by the recurrent appearance and vanishing of "speranza" (hope). The madrigal "Or passata è la speranza" (Now hope has gone) most famously depicts the cycle, where the poet recalls the nourishment that hope once brought to her life, though now that it has disappeared, all comfort is lost.

Gambara's literary persona remains sensitive to the transience of earthly desires and is fundamentally distressed by the passage of time. Memory serves its conventional function as the poet's simultaneous refuge and prison, and poetry is the exclusive conduit through which she may attempt to relieve her emotional pain. The poems describe being led to the brink of death in this state, though conversely, death as an escape from the extreme pain of suffering is characterized as impossible. The madrigals "Quando sarà ch'io mora" (When will it be that I will die) and "Così estrema è la doglia" (So extreme is this pain) dramatize the poet's simultaneous desire for death and the impossibility of achieving it, while the sonnet "Quel nodo in cui la mia beata sorte" (That knot in which, [by Heaven's command,] my blessed fate) expresses the fear that ending her own life will deny her admission to heaven in the afterlife.

In some instances, Gambara depicts the root of this pain in the cruelty of the object of affection, but more frequently, the speaker is cast as the victim of offenses committed by the personified forces of "Amor" (Love), who takes the poet's heart prisoner, and "Fortuna" (Fortune), the figure responsible for depriving the poet of her beloved. Yet Gambara's poet-persona does not surrender unequivocally to defeat. Shining moments of rebellion occur against these forces that assault her emotional well-being, quite pronouncedly in the sonnet "Straziami a possa tua, crudel Fortuna" (Torture me with all your might, cruel Fortune), for example, where the poet taunts Fortune to assail her with merciless blows only to meet her resistance. By and large, the most recurrent trope in Gambara's love poems is separation from the beloved; we see it in the multiple iterations of the verb "privare" (deprive). The poet endures episodes of departure and periods of separation from her love, whom she longs for and with whom she imagines a future moment of reunion. Gambara's repeated play on absence, deprivation, and separation overlaps frequently with the quintessentially Petrarchan depiction of the beloved as a source of light, whereby the poet is frequently deprived of the "luce" (light) that emanates from the object of her affection. The beloved-as-light trope features in a series of poems in which Gambara contemplates "occhi lucenti e belli" (shining and lovely eyes). In these compositions, the melancholic tone shifts to present the eyes as an uplifting, life-giving force, leading the poet to experience moments of elation in love:

> Dal veder voi, occhi lucenti e chiari,
> nasce un piacer ne l'alma, un gaudio tale
> ch'ogni sdegno, ogni affanno, ogni gran male
> soavi tengo, e chiamo dolci e cari.
>
> (At the sight of you, eyes shining and bright, such joy springs forth in my soul that every dismay, every labor, every great pain I consider gentle and call sweet and dear.)

Throughout Gambara's love poetry one finds references to the landscape and the environment as they correspond to the emotional fluctuations in the verse. In other poems, place is the subject; in these idyllic meditations Gambara articulates an intimate and profoundly emotional connection to her surrounding land. A notable example is a four-stanza poem in ottava rima, "Con quel caldo desio che nascer sole" (With the warm desire that is oftimes born) [in the heart] commemorating her family's return to rule Brescia in 1532. Gambara opens the composition by expressing her devotion to her homeland in terms redolent of a reunion of two distant lovers. Following Petrarch's model, specifically his canzone 126 of the *Rerum vulgarium fragmenta*, Gambara fuses feelings of love with her meditation on the idyllic scenery, but in her politicized reshaping of the theme, the object of Gambara's desire *is* the landscape of her homeland. Gambara assuages the fulfillment of her amorous longing—a satisfaction that remains sublimated and frustrated throughout Petrarch's verse—by casting as the object of her affection her family's ruling domain, rather than a male love interest.

The poem recalls the relief felt when the beloved returns, so prevalent in the "occhi" poems of her love poetry, and affirms the echo with the lexical modification of the "occhi beati" (blessed eyes) of her youthful love poetry to the "lochi beati" (blessed places) of her homeland in the final stanza. This substitution allows Gambara to project the image of a chaste ruler who channels her desire for love through politics in her devotion to her family's political sovereignty. The poem imagines an earthly paradise, elevating her *patria* to a veritable golden age setting in an allusion to the instrumental role that Charles V—depicted as a modern-day Caesar in Gambara's political poetry—played in the restoration of the Gambara family's political power in the region.[62] This inventive transposition of love poetry to a politicized celebration of place speaks to Gambara's talent to tailor, rather than transgress, popular literary conventions to suit her needs as a political figure throughout the second phase of her literary career.

Gambara's innovative transformation of traditional lyric models, particularly that of Petrarch, is evident across her correspondence poetry. Gambara's 1529 sonnet to Pietro Bembo, "A l'ardente desio ch'ognor m'accende" (The burning desire that ever inspires me), is fittingly Petrarchan in style and thematic inspiration, destined for the by now acclaimed literary father and master of *petrarchismo*. Yet here, Gambara departs from the Petrarchan love theme to rehearse the conversion plot of the *Rerum vulgarium fragmenta*. In the sonnet, Gambara positions Bembo as the elevating spiritual guide, serving as the crucial factor in the confirmation of her desire to reinforce her faith fully and overcome all impediments blocking her way. The gender inversion flatters Bembo: he is, as Laura was for Petrarch, the one in control of "eterna fama e vera gloria" (eternal fame and true glory), while Gambara, in the male Petrarchan role, situates herself in the unthreatening position of disciple to Bembo's literary and moral example. Gambara turns her attention from Bembo to herself in the second half of the sonnet, where in definitive tones she proclaims that she has superseded her past state of mind, once occupied with low thoughts and desires—a reference to her production of love poetry in

62. Cox, *Women's Writing in Italy*, 68–69.

her youth—and now dedicates herself exclusively to an honorable and virtuous life.

The shift in Gambara's poet-persona, from a woman suffering in love to one who strives and achieves a virtuous existence, may be understood as a necessary transformation in self-fashioning impelled by her position as a widow regent. Gambara's refashioning of her literary persona worked to reinforce her respectability as a female ruler. The public literary declaration of her unassailable virtue not only effectively countered the stereotype of women's fickle sexual nature that might have compromised her credibility as a single female ruler, but also established a public portrait of herself as a pious widow. Gambara's overt manifestation of her virtue, and more subtle declaration of her chastity by erasing the presence of love in her poetry, would have served the political purpose of moderating any potential tensions surrounding her as a female ruler.

A further innovation in Gambara's approach to the Petrarchan model in her mature verse is found where she writes of love by proxy. These sonnets present a triangular narrative framework, whereby Gambara separates the artist from her subject, traditionally fused in Petrarch's verse, and posits herself at a distance, writing about another couple's amorous intrigue. This authorial perspective allowed Gambara to speak of Petrarchan love and loss in a manner that avoids any display of a first-person connection—a poetic posture that effectively protected her public image as a chaste widow. Gambara employed the paradigm in sonnets to Bembo and Pietro Aretino, to speak of their beloveds, respectively, but the most intriguing use of this triangulated structure may be found in the series of sonnets Gambara composed between 1543 and 1544 for the Marchese del Vasto Alfonso d'Avalos and his wife, Maria d'Aragona.[63] These sonnets relate the domestic drama of d'Aragona's suffering while her husband is away at war, while Gambara implicitly alludes to her own past familiarity with the worries that occupy the mind of a consort to a military general.

Gambara's depiction of the distinctly feminine plight of enduring the absence of the husband away at war and her dramatization of the incompatibilities of war and marriage recall Vittoria Colonna's "Epistola"—a letter-poem in terza rima written to her husband while

63. Gambara, *Le rime*, 91–93.

he was fighting at the battle of Ravenna in 1512.[64] Gambara's positioning of her own poem as following the literary precedent of Colonna's provides a subtle, yet persuasive means to achieve a positive reception of her verse, and in turn, secure her standing in the powerful Colonna family's political favor. The first two sonnets written for d'Avalos emphasize their femininity of speech, as Gambara projects into direct discourse d'Aragona's innermost thoughts and feelings, while d'Avalos, silent, must listen to the cries of his wife: "E 'l mio Davalo, forse intento sempre / con l'armi e con l'ingegno a render vano / il nemico furor, di me non cura?" (Maybe my d'Avalos, always intent to defeat the enemy frenzy with the force of arms and intellect, does not care about me?) The third and final sonnet in the sequence is for Maria d'Aragona, and it follows Colonna's framing of the plight of women at a time of war as its own warlike experience, raising women to heroic status, as Gambara posits d'Aragona as a woman of infinite strength.

A unique instance of Gambara's mature oeuvre that departs from these innovative maneuvers within the Petrarchan sonnet form is the twenty-seven-stanza poem composed in ottava rima, "Quando miro la terra, ornata e bella" (When I behold the beautiful land, bountifully adorned). The narrative poem articulates three major themes: Gambara opens with a contemplation of the fleetingness of time and human mortality; she laments the moral decay of tyrants and court rulers consumed with material possession and power; and she extols the practice of virtue to call back to the earth the coveted golden age through a meditation on the pastoral ideal. Fabrizio Luna published this poem in the index of his *Vocabolario* in 1536, though after this publication, the poem was misattributed to Vittoria Colonna throughout the sixteenth century.[65] A further critical tension surrounding the poem is the uncertainty of its dedicatee. The

64. The "Epistola" was published in the appendix of a *Vocabolario* by Fabrizio Luna where Gambara's stanza poem "Quando miro la terra, ornata e bella" was also included. See Bullock's edited version of Gambara's poetry: Gambara, *Le rime*, 37. Colonna's poem primarily models Ovid's *Heroides* (5 BCE), though there was a developing genre of male-authored epistolary narratives expressing a first-person feminine voice beginning with Niccolò da Correggio's letter poem, in which he supposes the voice of his wife to lament his imprisonment by the Venetians in 1482–83. For a study of Colonna's "Epistola" see Carlo Vecce, "Vittoria Colonna: Il codice epistolare della poesia femminile," *Critica letteraria* 21 (1993): 3–34.

65. Gambara, *Le rime*, 37, 129.

hypothesis that Gambara dedicated her poem to Cosimo I de' Medici (1519–74) recurs throughout the critical tradition, but the position remains problematic because the poem was printed in October 1536 and Cosimo did not come to power in Florence until after an unexpected turn of events—the unforeseen assassination of Alessandro de' Medici (1510–37)—in January 1537.[66] What remains beyond doubt is that Gambara's poem conveys support for the legacy of Medici rule in Florence through her evocation of the golden age protected by the flourishing Medici family. In the penultimate stanza, Gambara recalls the age of Lorenzo "il Magnifico" de' Medici by employing his distinct imagery of the evergreen laurel that served as a metaphor to represent the perpetual prosperity of Medici family rule:

> [D]ico di voi, o de l'altera pianta
> felice ramo del ben nato Lauro,
> in cui mirando sol si vede quanta
> virtù risplende dal mar Indo al Mauro,
> e sotto l'ombra gloriosa e santa
> non s'impara aprezar le gemme o l'auro
> ma le grandezze ornar con la virtute,
> cosa da far tutte le lingue mute.
>
> (I speak of you, happy branch of the proud plant, the nobly born Laurel. Just looking at you one sees all the

66. The dedication of the poem to Cosimo I de' Medici first appears in print in a collection of Gambara's verse from 1851. See Gambara, *Le rime*, 31–32. Bullock, who edited this collection, also attributes the dedication of the poem to Cosimo I de' Medici, ibid., 155. In Gambara's biographical tradition, the dedication of the poem to Cosimo I de' Medici begins with Zamboni, where he states on p. 50: "[A] Cosimo I gran Duca di Toscana indirizzò le bellissime ottave sopra l'instabilità della presente vita" (to Cosimo I grand Duke of Tuscany [she] addressed the beautiful octaves on the instability of this present life), Zamboni, "Vita di Veronica Gambara." Later commentaries on Gambara's life and poetry similarly attribute the poem as dedicated to Cosimo I de' Medici. See Chimenti, *Veronica Gambara*, 54; Clementia de Courten, *Veronica Gambara: Una gentildonna del Cinquecento* (Milan: Casa Editrice "Est," 1935), 35; Giovanni Macchia, "Quattro poetesse del Cinquecento," *Rivista rosminiana* 31, no. 20 (1937): 156; Claudio Vela, "Poesia in musica," 412; Rinaldina Russell, ed., *Italian Women Writers: A Bio-Bibliographical Sourcebook* (Westport, CT: Greenwood Press, 1994), 147.

> virtue that shines from the Indian to the Moorish sea, and under your glorious and saintly shade one learns not how to value gold and jewels, but how to adorn greatness with virtue—something that could silence every tongue.)

Gambara extends the metaphor of Lorenzo's "nobly born Laurel" to praise the virtue of the descendent ("the happy branch") stemming from "the proud plant" to assert the organic, natural origin of Medici family rule in the legacy of Lorenzo de' Medici. Gambara supported the 1530 campaign of Charles V and Clement VII to return the Medici family to the government of Florence, and her son Ippolito likely served in the imperial army for the cause. Broadly, the emperor was seeking to stabilize Medici control, while Gambara's expression of hope for the continuation of the Medici dynasty under the spirit of the golden age of Lorenzo conveyed her steadfast support for Charles V's cause.

Gambara's sonnets on Charles V are spoken in the voice of a solemn and erudite ruler, vigilantly invested in the expression of the iconography surrounding Charles V's developing empire and intent on harmonizing the eminence of her subject with her own grave and elevated style. The sonnets draw heavily on Charles V's imperial *concetto* as it circulated throughout the northern Italian court culture. In "Guida con la man forte al camin dritto" ([Lord,] guide with a strong hand toward the right path), Gambara assumes the voice of the collective Christian population; the war against the Ottoman Empire is presented in terms of its universal significance to Christianity and is likened to the liberation of the Jewish people in Egypt, and to the wars of Caesar Augustus. The evocation of these biblical and historical subtexts points to a shift in Gambara's mature oeuvre to produce sonnets with loftier allusions. In the execution of this more elevated style, Gambara continued to adhere to the Petrarchan lyric and linguistic forms authorized by Bembo in his *Prose della volgar lingua* (1524) by producing, as did Bembo, an effect of *gravità* in place of *piacevolezza*.[67]

67. For neo-Latin poetry in sixteenth-century Italy, see Andrea Afribo, *Teoria e prassi della "gravitas" nel Cinquecento* (Florence: Franco Cesati, 2001); Emilio Bigi, *Poesia latina e volgare nel Rinascimento* (Naples: Morano, 1989); Stefano Carrai, *I precetti di Parnaso: Metrica*

We see this shift in weight in Gambara's rhyme scheme in the positioning of longer syllables with double consonants as the last word of almost each line, effectively slowing the pace of the sonnet:

> Guida con la man forte al camin dritto,
> Signor, le genti Tue ch'armate vanno
> per dar a' Tuoi nemici acerbo danno
> e per Tua Gloria a far Cesare invitto.
>
> (Lord, guide with a strong hand toward the right path your people who charge forward in arms, to bring bitter harm upon your enemies and, in the name of your glory, to keep Caesar unvanquished.)

The lens through which the political poems view the emperor indicate Gambara was familiar with erudite literary models. Indeed, in "Là dove più con le sue lucid'onde" (There, where [...] with its lucid waters), Gambara imagines the raising of a monument in commemoration of Charles V along the bank of the river Mella in her native Brescia, recalling thus the prologue to Virgil's *Georgics*, 3, where Virgil describes a monument to Caesar Augustus on the bank of the Mincio River in his native Mantua. Gambara's sonnets devoted to the theme of Charles V's empire present her most elevated and learned lyric production, and one may look to Gambara's political context—specifically in her aim to produce poetry that would maintain her favorable political relations with the emperor in light of his treatment of Correggio, Brescia, and her family at large—as having inspired this literary transformation.

---

e generi poetici nel Rinascimento italiano (Rome: Bulzoni, 1999); Daniel L. Heiple, *Garcilaso de la Vega and the Italian Renaissance* (University Park: Pennsylvania State University Press, 1994).

Aftermath of Writing

"Were there only more women on earth like you"
—Lucia Bertani dell'Oro

Gambara's self-fashioning as a woman of unassailable virtue extended naturally into the biographical tradition that followed her. The tone of reverence was set by Rinaldo Corso's luminous literary portrait in his *Vita di Veronica Gambara* of 1556, where he underscores Gambara's moral excellence in every turn.[68] Corso appropriately recognizes Gambara's accomplishment of securing Charles V's alliance and support for her small Correggio fiefdom, claiming that the emperor praised the countess for three qualities: "First for her virtue and renown. Next for her lineage, as the Correggio family is truly and legitimately connected to noble and ancient Austrian blood; and finally for being the sister of Lord Gambara."[69]

The depiction of Gambara's virtue as tightly bound to the name and repute of her family—both by birth within the Gambara family and by marriage to the Correggio line—ratifies the method with which Gambara fashioned her persona throughout her years as the Countess of Correggio, in her timely public alignment with the advancement of her elder brothers on the political landscape, and her steadfast promotion of her young sons in public office. Corso posits Gambara as one of the first women to emulate the Petrarchan model and anticipates her future as a "perpetua scorta" (enduring guide) for female poets to follow. Corso's title is fitting. Gambara's success came in the form of her perennial presence in published anthologies throughout the centuries—a publication history that accurately reflects the nature of Gambara's oeuvre in its range of thematic occupation and stylistic practice. It was not until 1759 that Gambara's poems were assembled in a single printed edition.[70] Even so, the praise of women poets of

68. Rinaldo Corso, "Vita di Veronica Gambara," in his *Vita di Giberto III da Correggio* (Ancona, 1566), in the collection of the Biblioteca Nazionale Centrale di Firenze.

69. "Prima per la virtù, & fama sua. Poi per essergli parenti; che i signori di Correggio sono del veri, & leggitimo, et antico sangue d'Austria. Et finalmente per essere ella sorella di Monsignor Gambara." Corso, "Vita di Veronica Gambara," n.p.

70. Gambara, *Rime e lettere di Veronica Gambara*, ed. Felice Rizzardi.

her own and subsequent generations, such as Laura Terracina, Lucia Bertani dell'Oro (quoted above), Luisa Bergalli, and Laura Battiferi, raised Gambara to iconic status as a model poet. We read Gambara today because the women of Gambara's day read her. While Gambara developed original rhetorical devices to court the approval and alliance of Italy's most powerful figures of her time, she ultimately drew the encomium of her contemporaries and predecessors, which gave rise to her legacy as a "Sappho" of the early sixteenth century.[71]

A Note on the Translation

Every translator is compelled, sooner or later, to choose between being as faithful as possible to the meaning of the source text, or privileging and trying to reproduce its formal aspects. Paola Ugolini, the cotranslator of this collection, and I decided to adhere as much as possible to the ideas expressed through the poems rather than to the form, especially given the density of meaning of Gambara's poetic language and the formal complexity of her Italian sentence structures. Therefore, we opted for a prose translation, which endeavors to be as faithful as possible to Gambara's elaborate and erudite style.

The grammatical structure of Gambara's poetry proved to be difficult because of her frequent use of qualifying clauses and phrases, reflecting the thoughtful rationality of her poetic language. Similarly challenging was her use of relative clauses, by which the subject is characterized through the gendered imagery surrounding it. Such constructions are related to the peculiar syntactic structure of Romance languages and would have been impossible to reproduce into English exactly. In these cases, we transformed the syntax into English common use, but always strove to reproduce the nuances implied in Gambara's word order choices. We also made an effort to reflect the logical emphasis of her sentences. We went formally farther from the original in the cases that compelled us to try to keep the logical structure of Gambara's thought, in some cases altering the grammatical subject of a clause to reflect the logical emphasis of the sentence.

Given that Italian has less lexical variety than English, picking the right sense for terms that can cover a variety of meanings in dif-

71. Cox, *Women's Writing in Italy*, 45.

ferent instances was also a challenge. We aimed to keep the nuances of the original Italian as much as possible. Some extra explanation had to be added in the translation in some very specific cases in order not to lose the multileveled meaning of some terms, as was the case, for example, in the terms of medieval and early modern philosophy—such as *ragione* and *intelletto*, *alma* and *spirito*—that were clear to the educated elites of the time, but risked being lost in translation to contemporary readers.

Of Gambara's extant oeuvre, we are able to date approximately half the compositions by the fact that they speak of historical events or were included in a dated letter. Given our inability to date the rest of the oeuvre precisely, we opted for a thematic grouping of the poems, rather than a chronological one. While some debate remains regarding the attribution of certain poems to Gambara, we followed Alan Bullock's catalogue of the poet's extant verse. One exception to this catalogue is our inclusion of the poem "Vinca gli sdegni" (May [the holy and sacred name of Christ overcome] your outrage), attributed to Colonna and not Gambara, though the publication history designates Gambara as the author of the sonnet. We made edits to the Italian text in instances in which the Italian grammatical structure appeared ambiguous, and we returned to the manuscript sources to guide these changes.

VERONICA GAMBARA
COMPLETE POEMS: A BILINGUAL EDITION

POEMS OF LOVE
POEMS OF PLACE
POEMS OF CORRESPONDENCE AND *ENCOMIA*
POLITICAL POEMS
SPIRITUAL POEMS
STANZE

POEMS OF LOVE

1

Essendo l'ora del partir mio gionta,
che non da te ma i' parto da me stessa,
da sì grave dolor l'alma è oppressa
che in pochi giorni io resterò defonta.
Ma nova pena al cor m'è sopragionta,
da un crudel dubio sol, lassa! processa,
qual fa che a morte, ahimè! più ognor appressa
questa mia vita con la tua congionta.
Il dubio che 'l mio cor afflige e preme
è che so te non mai aricordarti
di chi sempre per te languisce e geme;
onde ti mando i guanti tuoi per darti
memoria di chi è gionto a l'ore estreme
per troppo lagrimar sol per lassarti.

The hour of my departure[1] has arrived, when I part not from you, but from myself. My soul is burdened by such intense pain that soon I will be dead.

Yet a new sorrow has befallen my heart—alas, it sprang from a sole, cruel doubt—and now this life of mine, so closely bound to yours, nears death by the hour.

The worry weighing on my heart is that I know you never remember the one who always yearns and cries for you.[2]

Thus, I send your gloves[3] as a remembrance of her who came to her final hours, owing to the many tears shed solely for having to part from you.

1. The drama of departure from the beloved is recurrent throughout Gambara's love poetry, where she (in the persona of poet) writes predominantly of the pain of separation in love rather than of the joy felt by lovers in union. The trope of departure and separation reveals the influence of Petrarch in Gambara's early poetry, recalling as it does Petrarch's state of perpetual separation from Laura throughout the *Rerum vulgarium fragmenta*. Here Gambara describes an inner division of the soul as it separates from the beloved.

2. The fear of being forgotten by the beloved inverts Petrarch's fear of not being able to fully recall the memory of Laura. For other poems that express the fear of loss of the beloved through a lapse of memory or a failure to be loyal, see poems 4 and 7.

3. It is unclear if the sonnet is intended for a specific recipient, and thus if the act of sending the beloved a pair of gloves should be read literally or figuratively.

2

Non bastava ad Amor empio e fallace
avermi priva del tuo sacro volto,
senza 'l quale essendo io è da me tolto
ogni mio ben, ogni contento e pace,
che, ancor per crescer più l'ardente face
non mi lassò mostrarti il male accolto
pel tuo partir nel cor, né come involto
fosse per tal effetto in duol tenace.
Ma, poiché Amor crudel non volse, allora
con questa mia piangendo e 'l dico e scrivo
esser te sol colui che 'l cor adora,
e, benché quel sia del vederti privo,
d'altro ch'a te pensar non vive ognora,
e 'n tal stato ha a restar perfin ch'io vivo.

It was not enough for pitiless and deceptive Love to deprive[4] me of your sacred face, without which I am robbed of every joy, happiness, and peace,

but to intensify the burning flame, Love did not let me show you the pain gathered in my heart because of your departure,[5] nor how for such reason it was enfolded in unceasing agony.

Since this was not cruel Love's desire, now I weep as I sing through my verse that you are the only one my heart adores,

and though denied the sight of you, it lives only by thinking of you, and in this state it must remain as long as I live.[6]

4. The "privare" trope expands the theme of separation from the beloved. See also poem 4.

5. See note 1.

6. This refrain is reminiscent of the final stanza of Petrarch's canzone 127 in *Rerum vulgarium fragmenta*, where the thought of Laura is the only thing that sustains him, so close to death does he feel in her absence.

3[7]

Quando sarà ch'io mora,
Amor, se 'n questa cruda dipartita
non può tanto dolor finir mia vita?
Qualor avien ch'io pensi
quel che dir mi volea l'ultimo sguardo
e 'l partir lento e tardo,
con quei sospir sì accensi,
come pon star in me l'anima e i sensi?
S'allor ch'io gli odii dire
quell'ultime parole in tanto ardore
non mi s'aperse il core,
e non potei morire,
quando potrò mai più di vita uscire?
Io n'uscirò, ch'a tant'aspro martire
non potrò già durar, vedermi priva
e sì lungi da lui, e che sia viva!

When will it be that I will die, Love, if in this cruel departure[8] so much pain cannot end my life?

Whenever I happen to imagine what his final glance sought to say, along with his slow, prolonged parting, with such fiery, loving sighs, how can my soul and senses remain within me?[9]

If in the moment I heard him utter those final words with such passion, my heart did not split open and I was unable to die, when will I ever be able to leave this life?

I will leave it, for I can no longer endure such torment: to see myself without him, so far from him, and yet still alive!

7. Madrigal.

8. See note 1.

9. The poem describes the division of the soul in separation as it seeks to maintain union with the absent beloved. There's an echo here of Petrarch, *Rerum vulgarium fragmenta* 329.2–4, "o fido sguardo, or che volei tu dirme, / partend'io per non esser mai contento?" (O faithful glance, oh, what did you wish to tell me when I departed, never to be happy again?). *Petrarch's Lyric Poems: The "Rime sparse" and Other Lyrics*, ed. and trans. Robert M. Durling (Cambridge, MA: Harvard University Press, 1976). All references to and quotations from Petrarch's *Rerum vulgarium fragmenta* in these footnotes are taken from this edition. Cf. poem 20; see also note 53.

4[10]

Amor: poich'io son priva
de l'alma vista in cui mia vita giace
dammi almen qualche pace,
acciò ch'in tanto duol possa star viva!
Fa' che l'alta speranza che nutriva
miei spiriti tristi 'nanzi la partita
non abandoni il core,
che, pien di grave ardore,
senza lei non porria tenersi in vita,
ma con l'aiuto suo spera far tanto
che starà vivo, benché in doglia e in pianto.
E se lontan dal bel mio lume santo
pur debb'io star fa che la data fede
non mi sia rotta mai,
che a 'sti miei crudi guai
né al mio languir dimando altra mercede;
ma se mancar mi dee fa almen ch'insieme
la vita manchi e le mie doglie estreme.

Love: since I am deprived[11] of the noble sight in which my life resides, give me at least some respite, so that in such agony I may stay alive.

Let not the high hope that nourished my lowly spirits before his departure[12] abandon my heart that, so full of painful passion, without hope cannot survive; but with her[13] help, it hopes to be able to stay alive, even if in tears and sorrow.

If I must remain far from my beautiful, sacred light,[14] may his devotion to me never waver,[15] as I ask no other mercy for my harsh

10. Madrigal.

11. See note 4.

12. See note 1.

13. The "her" is in reference to "hope."

14. The image of the object of affection as a body of light follows Petrarch's depiction of Laura throughout the *Rerum vulgarium fragmenta*. See also Gambara's poem 24.4: "bel lume santo." This phrase can be found also in Colonna's poetry, in reference to her husband. Gambara's poem was likely composed long before she knew of Colonna; their shared use of the image reveals Petrarch's influence on both poets.

15. See note 2.

woes, nor for my yearning; but should his loyalty vanish, may my life and my extreme pains[16] disappear with it.

16. The phrase "doglie estreme" occurs in two other love poems, see 5.1 and 26.12.

5[17]

Così estrema è la doglia
ch'a così estremo mal mal non arriva,
e a questo modo me ne resto viva.
Sarei ben morta, omai,
ma 'l dolor ch'ho nel cor, sì grave e forte,
non dà loco a la morte,
né accrescer può né sminuir miei guai.
Ahi, dispietata offesa!
Come farò diffesa
se m'hai sì pien d'angoscia l'alma e 'l petto
che fuor non può spirar l'anima accesa
e vivo al mio dispetto?
Ma fra tutti i martir quest'è il maggiore:
non potermi doler del mio dolore!

So extreme is this pain[18] that no evil can reach such an evil, and in this manner I stay alive.

I would be well dead by now, but the pain held deep in my heart, so heavy and strong, does not yield to death, and can neither increase nor diminish my woes.

Alas, pitiless offense! How can I mount a defense, if you filled my soul and breast with such anguish that my burning soul cannot exhale from my body, and I live in spite of my own self?

But of all the torments, this is the greatest: to be unable to grieve over my own grief.[19]

17. Madrigal.

18. See note 16.

19. The speaker's pain comes from not being able to express her emotions. She is silent because she must conceal her feelings, not because she cannot find the proper poetic expression.

6

Più volte il miser cor avea assaltato
Amor, né mai potendo averne onore,
ma sempre ritrovando il suo vigore
forte, talché di speme era privato;
onde, essendo esso un giorno assai turbato,
usando ogni sua forza e ogni valore
deliberò aver prigione il core,
e poi tenerlo in eterno legato.
Così gli riuscì che i fati rei,
ponendo inanzi a me tuo sacro aspetto,
posono in servitù gli spirti mei;
da indi in qua l'imagin tua nel petto
porto scolpita, talché dove sei
sempre è la mente mia con l'intelletto.

Many times Love assailed my miserable heart, though never able to acquire victory, always finding its vigor strong, so that Love was deprived of hope.

Wherefore one day, finding himself in distress, using all his strength and force, Love resolved to take my heart prisoner and keep it bound for eternity.

Love so succeeded that the cruel Fates,[20] placing your sacred image before me, confined my spirits to servitude.

From that day forward I carry your likeness engraved in my breast,[21] so that wherever you are, there are always my mind and my intellect.[22]

20. Love renders the poet a servant to Love and to the Fates. Cf. poems 8 and 16.

21. Petrarch, *Rerum vulgarium fragmenta*, 96.5–7, "Ma 'l bel viso leggiadro che depinto / porto nel petto et veggio ove ch'io miri" (But that lovely smiling face which I carry painted in my breast and see wherever I look).

22. Gambara is referring to the philosophy of love, originally explored in the poetry of Cavalcanti and Dante, and later elaborated by Bembo, in which love is bound to the intellect as an object of the intellect. See also poem 37.13–14.

7

Libra non son, né mai libra esser spero
dal crudel laccio ove già fui legata,
perché troppo mortal la piaga è stata
che già ferì mio cor puro e sincero.
Né libra mai sarò da un sol pensiero,
nel qual dì e notte sempre isto occupata,
che la mia libertà, qual t'ho donata,
non sprezzi, ahimè! tuo cor superbo e fiero.
Né libra da timor, né libra ancora
mai sarò da martir, da acerbe pene
che mi affligon per te, crudele, ognora.
Alfin né libra mai da tue catene
starò, crescendo in me più d'ora in ora
varie passion per te soavi e amene.

I am not free, nor do I ever wish to be free, from the cruel snare[23] where I was once bound, for the wound that injured my pure and honest heart was far too lethal.

I will never be free from the sole worry weighing on my thoughts day and night: alas, that my liberty, my gift to you, could be despised by your proud and disdainful heart![24]

I will never be free from fear, nor from torment, nor from the bitter pangs of grief that I constantly suffer because of you, oh cruel one.

In the end, I will never be free from your chains,[25] as so many sweet and alluring passions for you grow stronger within me by the hour.

23. The suffering experienced by the poet, in which she is caught in a stasis—in the trap of love without desire for escape—is Petrarchan in the sense that the poet is painfully aware of being weighed down by her willed contemplation of the object of affection. See sonnet 134 of the *Rerum vulgarium fragmenta* and especially sonnet 76: "e come vero prigioniero afflitto / de le catene mie gran parte porto" (and like a true suffering prisoner I carry a large part of my chains). Here the "laccio" and "catene" of Gambara's lines 2 and 12 draw on the Petrarchan lexicon of entrapment by love. See also Gambara's poem 9.1–4.

24. See note 2.

25. See note 23.

8

Amor: quanto i miei giorni aspri sian stati,
ed or più che mai sian, dir non tel voglio,
che 'l sai, e teco me ne dolsi e doglio,
sol per servir chi mi diè in sorte i fati,
ma, avendo in lui li miei pensier locati,
e ferma in adorarlo qual dur scoglio,
sperava mitigar tuo fiero orgoglio,
ma vedo i van disegni esser fallati,
ché ognor ti sforzi, con crudeli inganni,
congionger a' miei dì aspro e dur stento
per far che lunghi sian miei crudi affanni;
che, se un diaspro allegerì il tormento,
per esser di chi fu non i miei danni
cessati son ma più aspri ad ogn'or sento.

Love: I do not want to say how bitter my days have been, and how now they are even more so, for you already know, and to you I complained and still complain only because I serve the one whom the fates bestowed upon me.[26]

But as I centered my thoughts on him and stood solid as a rock in my adoration, I hoped to mitigate your fierce pride;

now I see my vain plans are flawed, for you still strive with cruel deceits to bind my days to bitter hardship so my harsh troubles will carry on.

Even if a crystal[27] could alleviate my torment, being from whom it came,[28] my woes do not cease, but are felt ever more bitter by the day.

26. See note 20.

27. The reference is to a gem or crystal with healing powers.

28. Because the gift was given by the beloved, the gift's affiliation with the object of affection would only bring further pain.

9

Quando Amor mi condusse a quel dur gioco,
dal qual partirmi, ahimè! non mai più spero,
donò per medicina al mal mio fero
speranza, ond'io vivea contenta in foco;
talché distanza mai, tempo, né loco
ebber forza scemar l'ardor mio vero,
che speme sol guidava il mio pensero,
talch'ogni gran martir mi parea poco.
Ed or ch'io mi credea viver felice,
e coglier di speranza il dolce frutto,
passata è la speranza, ahimè! infelice,
e 'l misero mio cor, arso e distrutto,
ardendo vive, e più, se 'l ver dir lice,
d'ogni ben privo e di speranza in tutto.

When Love led me to that cruel game from which, alas, I no longer hope to be free, he gave hope as medicine for my wound so I happily lived in flames.[29]

Neither distance, nor time, nor place had the power to abate my true ardor, for hope alone steered my thoughts to the point that every great torment seemed minor.

And once I believed that I could live in happiness, and that I was to reap the sweet fruit of hope, alas hope has gone,[30] unhappy me,

and my poor heart, scorched and exhausted, carries on in flames, and, if I can tell the truth, it is deprived of all hope and every joy.

29. See note 23.

30. The speaker's loss of hope is described also in poem 10, where "passata è la speranza" (hope has gone) serves as a refrain.

10[31]

Or passata è la speranza
che mi tenne un tempo ardendo;
ben mi duol, poiché comprendo
nulla cosa aver constanza.

Or passata è la speranza.

Questa ingrata un tempo in foco
m'ha tenuta pur sperando,
e prendendo il mal mio a gioco
m'ha lassata lagrimando;
ed amando e desiando
mi condusse ognora a morte
con passion tenace e forte
e con più perseveranza.

Or passata è la speranza.

Mentre ch'ebbi lei per scorta
ogni mal mi parea leve;
senza, poi, smarrita e smorta,[32]
ogni poco mi par greve.
Lungo affanno e piacer breve
fin a qua sempre ho sentito;
per aver con sé servito
questo premio sol m'avanza.

Or passata è la speranza.

Io sperai, e quel sperare
mi nutriva in dolce fiama;
più non spero, e lagrimare
sol quest'alma desia e brama,

31. *Frottola-barzelletta.*

32. Rizzardi has *morta*—most likely a *lectio facilior* for *smorta*. Gambara, *Rime e lettere di Veronica Gambara*, 57.

e la morte ognora chiama
per soccorso al suo dolore
perché senza speme è 'l core
che già fu sua dolce stanza.

Or passata è la speranza.

Mia soave[33] dolce speme
da me, dunque, si è fuggita,
e al partir ne porta insieme,
lassa! il cor la stanca vita,
talché, essendo sbigotita
e di speme al tutto priva,
non vivendo io resto viva
senza alfin nulla speranza.

Or passata è la speranza.

Now hope has gone,[34] the hope that for a while kept me burning; now I truly hurt, as I understand that nothing in life is constant.

Now hope has gone.

For a time this ungrateful one[35] kept me aflame, yet hoping; and taking my pain as amusement, she abandoned me in my weeping. As I loved and desired, time and again she led me to death, with tenacious passion and even stronger perseverance.

Now hope has gone.

While hope served as my guide, every great pain appeared light; without her, I am lost and withered, and every minor pain seems great.

Enduring pain and fleeting pleasure is all I have felt up to now; such is the only prize left to me for having served under her.

Now hope has gone.

I hoped, and my hoping nourished me in a sweet flame. Now I hope no more, my soul longs only to weep, and it calls out to death

33. The line reads "Mia *sorte* e dolce speme" in Bullock's edition. Edited here to *soave* following Rizzardi. Gambara, *Rime e lettere di Veronica Gambara*, 58.

34. The phrase "passata è la speranza" is also in poem 9.11.

35. "This ungrateful one" is in reference to "hope."

to relieve its pain, for my heart is bereft of hope, that once was hope's sweet home.

Now hope has gone.

My beloved sweet hope has forsaken me, alas! In leaving, my heart carries away my tired life, and I, dismayed, wholly deprived of hope, without living I stay alive, in the end with no hope at all.

Now hope has gone.

11[36]

Mentre l'alte promesse a mille a mille
con mentita pietà non m'ingannaro
furon le fiame mie dolci e tranquille,
e 'l dolor e 'l piacer corsero al paro.
Crebbero poi sì calde le faville,
sommerse il poco dolce il molt'amaro,
e sì corse l'infermo mio desio
che la speranza col tardar morio.

While the thousands of noble promises did not deceive me with feigned compassion, my passionate flames were sweet and calm as pain and pleasure evenly flowed. Then the sparks grew so hot, great bitterness overcame the lesser sweet, and my ailing desire ran so far ahead that hope was killed by delay.

36. *Strambotto* in ottava rima.

12[37]

Tosto che 'l sol si scopre in orïente
lagrimosa tempesta agli occhi sorge,
né perché si ricopra in occidente
tregua al mio lagrimar la doglia porge.
Splendan le stell'o sian dal giorno spente
sempre più vivo il pianto mio risorge;
o sia torbida l'ora o sia tranquilla
in mestissimo umor l'alma si stilla.

As soon as the sun reveals itself in the east, a tearful storm surges from my eyes; nor, when it disappears in the west, does pain offer respite to my weeping. Whether the stars shine, or are extinguished by the day, my weeping resurges ever more alive; whether the hour be turbulent or tranquil, my soul drips sad waters.

37. *Strambotto* in ottava rima.

13

Ride la terra, e d'ogni parte rende
mille soavi e dilettosi odori;
coperta di leggiadri e vaghi fiori
a guisa d'un bel ciel tutta risplende.
Amor, ch'in tal stagion forza riprende,
rinova in ogni cor gli antichi amori,
e mille cari e leggiadretti ardori
d'ogni fedele amante in petto accende.
Scherzano per le piagge, lascivetti,
gli animai, l'un l'altro festeggiando,
ch'Amore insegna lor novi diletti;
sola io, d'ogni mia pace posta in bando,
offesa da timor, noie, e sospetti,
lontana dal mio ben vivo penando.

The earth smiles and yields far and wide myriad gentle sweet-scented fragrances; blanketed by delightful and delicate flowers, it shines forth as a glorious heaven.

Love, restoring his strength in that season,[38] renews old loves in every heart and ignites thousands of lovely little flames in the breast of each faithful lover.

Playing together throughout the land, happy wanton animals celebrate as Love teaches them new delights;

but I, alone, exiled from every peace, wounded by fear, woe, and worry, far from my good, live enshrouded in pain.

38. The renewal of love in spring is evoked to illuminate the speaker's despair in not being able to partake in the general flowering of love inspired by the season, as made clear in the final tercet. Petrarch first saw Laura in the month of April, so the theme occurs frequently in *Rerum vulgarium fragmenta*. Gambara's language closely echoes sonnet 310: "Zefiro torna, e 'l bel tempo rimena" (Zephyrus returns and leads back the fine weather). For other uses of the trope in Gambara; see poems 14.8–10 and 43.7–8.

14[39]

Da chi debbo sperar mai tregua o pace
se quel ch'agli altri giova
a me sol nuoce, mi consuma e sface?
Il tempo si suol dir che l'aspre pene
e li cocenti ardori
se non in tutto allegerisse alquanto,
ma ahi, lassa! in me tutt'il contrario aviene,
ch'al rinovar dei fiori
rinova i vecchi amori,
e in compagnia di lor la doglia e 'l pianto.
Qual sia dunque il mio stato acerbo e quanto
sia il mio constante amore,
quanta sia la mia fede,
più nol dirò poiché sì chiar si vede.

From whom can I ever expect truce or peace, if what brings comfort to others only harms, consumes, and destroys me?

It is said that time may relieve bitter pains and burning flames, if not entirely, at least in part.

Alas, in me the contrary comes to pass, so that upon the rebirth of flowers time renews old loves, and with them pain and sorrow.[40]

Thus, how bitter my state is, how much constant love I have, however much faith, I will say no more, for it is so clearly seen.

39. Madrigal.

40. See note 38.

15

Poiché Fortuna volse farmi priva
di te, Signor mio car, deh! tolto almeno
m'avesse la memoria, che 'l cor pieno
tien de' martiri che da lei deriva.
Che dich'io, stolta? senza lei non viva
sarei, perché, pensando a quello ameno
piacer ond'io mi pasco e vengo meno,
se ben mi spinge in mar può trarmi a riva.
La memoria mantienmi e mi disface;
la memoria mi fa lieta e scontenta;
ne la memoria il ben e 'l mal mio iace.
La memoria m'allegra e mi tormenta;
dunque da la memoria ho guerra e pace,
e in tal variar lei sola mi contenta.

Since Fortune wanted to deprive me of you, my lord, if only she could have taken my memory! Memory keeps my heart full of torments that derive from her.

What am I saying, foolish me? Without memory I would not be alive, for as I think of that sweet pleasure that nourishes and weakens me, memory sends me out to sea, yet it can draw me back to shore.

Memory preserves and destroys me; memory makes me happy and sad; in memory lies my good and my bad.

Memory gladdens and torments me; from memory I have war and peace, and in this variation, only she pleases me.

16

Poscia che 'l mio destin fermo e fatale
vuol ch'io pur v'ami, e che per voi sospiri,
quella pietà nel petto amor v'inspiri
che conviene al mio duol grave e mortale,
e faccia che 'l voler vostro sia uguale
agli amorosi ardenti miei desiri;
poi cresca quanto vuol doglia e martiri,
che più d'ogni altro ben dolce fia il male.
E se tal grazia impetro, almo mio sole,
nessun più lieto o glorïoso stato
diede Amor o Fortuna al mondo mai;
e quanti per adietro affanni e guai
patito ha il cor, ond'ei si dolse e duole,
chiamerà dolci, e lui sempre beato.

Since my fixed and fatal destiny[41] desires that I continue to love and sigh for you, may Love inspire in your breast a pity suited to my heavy and mortal sorrow.

May he accord your will with my burning amorous desires; then torment and pain may grow as they please, for such woe will be sweeter than any joy.

Should I be granted such mercy, my life-giving sun,[42] neither Love nor Fortune would have ever bestowed a state more joyful or glorious to this world;

and however many troubles my heart has suffered, for which it ached and still aches, it will call them sweet and live forever blessed.

41. See note 20.

42. This is another example of the object of affection as a source of light. The image is from Petrarch, *Rerum vulgarium fragmenta*, 188, "Almo sol" (Life-giving sun). For other instances of the beloved as sun in Gambara's love poetry, see poems 22.2, 25.3, and 26.13.

17

Straziami a possa tua crudel Fortuna,
e di me gioco fa quanto a te piace!
Godi del strazio mio, crudo[43] e fallace,
e giorno e notte in me martiri aduna!
Fa pur ch'io stenti e che mai tregua alcuna
non trovi al mio dolor troppo tenace!
Dammi pur sempre guerra e non mai pace,
e quanti mali hai teco in me raduna,
che forza non arai, mentre ch'io vivo,
muovere il fermo cor da quel pensiero
che mille volte il dì l'uccide e avviva!
Né temo il colpo tuo spietato e fiero,
che la cagione onde 'l mio mal deriva
tal è ch'ogni gran duol tengo leggiero!

Torture me with all your might, cruel Fortune; mock me as you please! Delight in my cruel and fallacious torment; amass suffering in me day and night!

Make me toil, and may my persevering pain never find respite! Always give me war, never peace; gather within me all the ills you possess,

for as long as I am alive, you will never have the strength to move my firm heart away from the thought that kills and revives it a thousand times a day.

I fear not your fierce, merciless blow, for the reason of my suffering is that I deem every great pain light!

43. A different interpretation may be to consider "crudo" (masculine singular) an error for "cruda" (feminine singular), as the poet is addressing Fortune, which is feminine in Italian.

18

Sciogli le trecce d'oro e d'ogni intorno
cingi le tempie de' tuoi mirti e allori,
Venere bella, e teco i santi Amori
faccian concordi un dolce almo soggiorno;
e tu, sacro Imeneo, cantando intorno,
di vaghe rose e di purpurei fiori,
col plettro d'oro in versi alti e sonori
rendi onorato questo altero giorno.
E voi tutti, o gran dei, che de' mortali
sete al governo, a man piena spargete
gioia, pace, dolcezza, amore, e fede,
acciò che i casti baci e l'ore liete
spese tra due siano felici, e tali
che dar non possa il Cielo altra mercede.

Loosen your golden tresses, adorn your head with your myrtles and laurels, beautiful Venus,[44] and let the saintly Loves happily linger with you.

And you, sacred Hymen,[45] as you wander around singing, with your golden plectrum in high sonorous verses, you honor this proud day with lovely roses and bright red flowers.

And you, great gods reigning over the mortals, spread with full hands[46] joy, peace, sweetness, love, and faith,

so the chaste kisses and happy hours spent between two lovers may be so full of joy that Heaven could give no greater reward.

44. Venus, Roman goddess of love.

45. Hymenaios, Greek god of marriage. The evocation of Hymen suggests that the sonnet marks the occasion of a wedding, perhaps that of Brunoro Gambara, the poet's brother, to Virginia Sanvitale Pallavacina in 1529.

46. The image of the shower of flowers may be drawn from Virgil, *Aeneid*, 6.883, the "Manibus, o, date lilia plenis" (give lilies, oh, with full hands) proclaimed by Anchises in honor of the deceased Marcellus, quoted in Dante, *Purgatorio*, 30.21, at the moment of Beatrice's arrival, and evoked in Petrarch's canzone 126. While in Virgil the phrase is a lamentation, in this poem it is clearly celebratory (as in Dante), as Gambara seeks to endow the occasion with divine grace and favor. Here flowers signal the birth of love; in other poems Gambara evokes the flourishing of love in springtime to contrast the poet's expressed despair in the absence of the beloved. Cf. poems 13 and 14 on this theme. The above quote, and all others from this work that appear in these notes, are from the following edition: Virgil, *Aeneid*, ed. and trans. Allen Mandelbaum (New York: Bantam Books, 1971).

19[47]

Se, quando per Adone o ver per Marte
arse Venere bella,
stato fossi, Signor, visto da lei,
quella ardente facella
sol per te, che di lor più degno sei,
arsa e accesa l'avrebbe in ogni parte,
perché ne l'arme il bellicoso Marte
vinci d'assai, e di bellezza Adone
cede al tuo paragone;
dunque se 'l Ciel t'aspira e fa immortale
meraviglia non è, perché sei tale.

If when beautiful Venus[48] burned with desire for Adonis[49] or for Mars,[50] had you, Lord, been seen by her,

that flame would have set her wholly ablaze solely for you,[51] for you are even more worthy than they.

For in arms you easily overcome the warlike Mars, and in beauty Adonis cedes in comparison.

So if Heaven desires you and renders you immortal, it is no wonder, for such you are.

47. Madrigal.

48. Venus, Roman goddess of love.

49. Adonis, a mortal beloved of Aphrodite, the Greek goddess of love.

50. Mars, Roman god of war.

51. The emphasis on the distinguished military abilities of the beloved suggests the subject of the poem could be Gambara's husband, Giberto Gambara, a military *condottiere.*

20

Quel nodo, in cui la mia beata sorte
per ordine del Ciel legommi e strinse,
con grave mio dolor sciolse e devinse
quella crudel che 'l mondo chiama Morte,
e fu l'affano sì gravoso e forte
che tutti i miei piaceri a un tratto estinse,
e, se non che ragione alfin pur vinse,
fatto avrei mie giornate e brevi e corte.
Ma tema sol di non andar in parte
troppo lontana a quella ove 'l bel viso
risplende sopra ogni lucente stella
mitigato ha 'l dolor, che 'ngeno od arte
far nol potea, sperando in Paradiso
l'alma veder oltra le belle bella.

That knot in which, by Heaven's command, my blessed fate bound and fastened me, to my great dismay, was untied and released by the cruelty that the world calls Death.[52]

The anguish was so extreme and strong that it extinguished every pleasure in an instant, and had reason not managed to prevail, I would have made my days brief and short.

But the sole fear of going to a place far from where[53] the lovely face shines brighter than every brilliant star

mitigated my pain, as intelligence and art could not, for I hope to see in Paradise the most beautiful among the beautiful souls.

52. The date of composition of this sonnet is not known, but the content suggests Gambara is speaking of the death of her husband, Giberto Gambara, in 1529. The reference to the knot of love that death unties recalls Petrarch's sonnet 271: "L'ardente nodo ov'io fui, d'ora in ora / contando, anni ventuno interi preso / Morte disciolse" (That burning knot in which I was hour by hour caught for twenty-one whole years, Death has untied).

53. As the poet contemplates suicide, she fears that punishment in the afterlife would place her in hell, far from her beloved in paradise. The fear of damnation after a suicide to cut short grief is expressed by Petrarch in canzone 71 of the *Rerum vulgarium fragmenta*, "Ma se maggior paura / non m'affrenasse, via corta et spedita / trarrebbe a fin questa aspra pena et dura" (But if a greater fear did not rein me in, a short and speedy way would bring to an end this bitter and hard suffering). Contrast the poet's earlier appeals for death to relieve her of suffering in absence of the beloved, as in poem 3.

21

Vaghi pensier, ch'al mesto ed arso core
sol sete cibo e sue fidate scorte:
da poi ch'ogn'altro ben tolmi mia sorte
a voi del viver mio resta l'onore.
Potran ben mia fortuna ingiusta, e Amore
non men di lei, straziarmi insino a morte,
ma non potran mai far che non stia forte,
mercè di voi, a l'empio suo furore,
ch'a malgrado di lor, dolci pensieri,
da voi ricevo vita, e per voi passo
sicura i più dubiosi e aspri sentieri;
per voi tengo alto il stato mio sì basso
né di Fortuna temo i colpi fieri,
ch'al dispetto di lei d'amar non lasso.

Beautiful thoughts, sole sustenance and faithful guide to my melancholy, burned-up heart: ever since my fate[54] robbed me of all other joy, the honor of my living remains yours.

Unjust Fortune, and Love no less than she, can well torment me to the brink of death, but they will never make it so that I, thanks to you, cannot stand strong before Fortune's pitiless fury,

for in spite of them, sweet thoughts, from you I gain life, and through you I safely pass over the most uncertain and difficult paths.[55]

Because of you I hold my lowly state high, and fear not the fierce blows of Fortune, for I never cease to love despite her.

54. The reference to "fate" here likely signifies the untimely death of Gambara's husband. Here she is not tortured by memory of the beloved, as she is when speaking of the drama of separation (see poem 15). Rather, the "beautiful" and "sweet" thoughts serve to sustain her against the cruel blows of Fortune. Cf. poem 20.

55. Petrarch, *Rerum vulgarium fragmenta*, 70.21–22, "Vaghi pensier che così passo passo / scorto m'avete a ragionar tant'alto" (Yearning thoughts, which thus step by step have led me to such high speech).

22

Di quel fido pensier, che mi conduce
sovente a contemplare il mio bel sole,
e a farmi odire il suon de le parole
che furno[56] al carcer mio fidato duce,
farmi potessi con la viva luce
veder cui non veder mi pesa e duole,
e dirgli le mie pene al mondo sole
come fa chi temendo amore induce.
Allor potrei sicuramente dire:
«Non è stato del mio più lieto in terra,
né ben mortale agguaglia il mio gioire!»
Ma dai crudi pensier, che mi fan guerra,
non trovo altro piacer se non morire,
ed un dolor ch'ogni speranza atterra.

If only I could, with the true light of that loyal thought—which often leads me to contemplate my beautiful sun[57] and to hear the sound of the words that served as my faithful guide in prison—

make myself visible to the one whom not seeing burdens and pains me,[58] and tell him my sufferings unmatched in the entire world, as does one who, in fear, is moved by Love.

Then I would be able to safely say: "No state on earth is more joyful than mine; no mortal good can compare to my rejoicing!"

But from the cruel thoughts warring within me, I receive no pleasure other than death, and a sorrow that strikes down every hope.

56. Variation on *furono*.

57. See note 42.

58. The pain is a result of not seeing the beloved.

23

Da indi in qua ch'agli occhi miei si tolse
vostra luce, del mondo eterno onore,
da me fuggendo il tormentato core
gioioso a seguir voi tutto si volse.
Né un punto sol di lassar me si dolse,
preso dal vostro divo almo splendore,
e, invaghito di quel, subito fore
volò, che indietro mai non si rivolse.
Con voi dimora e dal bel vostro volto
il viver prende, e ogn'altro cibo sprezza,
né cura d'altro ben poco né molto;
felice lui, che gusta la dolcezza
del parlar dolce, e non veder gli è tolto
l'alta leggiadra e singular bellezza!

From the moment your light[59] was taken from my eyes, eternal honor of the world, my tormented heart escaped from me and joyfully turned to follow you.[60]

Not once did it regret abandoning me, seized by your divine splendor, fully enamored, it flew off in an instant and never turned to look back.

My heart dwells with you and takes life from your lovely sight, scorning any other nourishment, and does not care for any other good, whether great or small.

Happy is my heart because it savors the sweetness of your sweet, pleasing speech, and is never denied the sight of your noble, graceful, and singular beauty.

59. The "light" signifies the beloved.

60. Here the heart escapes from the body to remain in union with the beloved. For similar imagery, see sonnet 313 of Petrarch's *Rerum vulgarium fragmenta*.

24

Quando fia mai quel dì, felice tanto,
ch'io dica: «Occhi miei mesti: or v'allegrate!
Ciechi omai più non sete! Orsù! Mirate
la dolce vista del bel lume santo!

Sorde mie orecchie: ora al celeste canto
e al suo dolce parlar attente state!
Lagrime amare e calde: or v'affrenate!
Ecco chi in allegrezza ha volto il pianto!»

Ahi, lasso! il mio desio tanto è possente
e sì debile e frale è la speranza
che di prima morir temo sovente!

E di temer sì avezza è per usanza
questa mia del suo mal presaga mente
che 'l van timor assai la speme avanza!

Will the happy day ever come when I can say: "Rejoice my sad eyes, for you are no longer blind! Come now, behold the sweet sight of the beautiful sacred light![61]

My deaf ears, listen now to the heavenly song and to his sweet speech! Warm bitter tears, cease your flow! Here is the one who turned my pain to joy!"

Alas, my desire is so powerful, and my hope so feeble and weak, that I often fear death will come before this day.[62]

And this mind of mine, so able to anticipate its own harm,[63] is so accustomed to fear that hope is overcome by fruitless dismay!

61. See note 14.

62. Here the poet emphasizes how weak her hope for reunion is, compared with her desire for it. A fear of dying from the weakness caused by separation before the joy of reunion can also be seen in poem 27.

63. Petrarch, *Rerum vulgarium fragmenta*, 314.1–2: "Mente mia, che presaga de' tuoi danni, / al tempo lieto già pensosa e trista" (O my mind, who, foreseeing your losses, already thoughtful and sad in the happy time).

25

«Occhi», dico talor, «orsù! godete!
ché 'l Ciel v'è pur nel mal benigno assai!
Dal vostro vivo sol splendon que' rai;
adunque il sguardo vostro in lor tenete!
E se stati gran tempo in pianto sete,
senza conforto alcun prender già mai,
lieti, lassate il pianto amaro omai,
n'ad altro ch'a gioir or attendete!
Se ragion è che dopo lunghi affanni
qualche breve riposo un'ora senta
col mirar sempre ristorate i danni;
e, pria che quella instabile si penta,
ricompensate», dico, «i mal spesi anni,
ché raro il Ciel al ben par che consenta!».

"Mine eyes," I often say, "now be glad, for even in your pain Heaven proves to be kind. Those rays shine down from your living sun,[64] so fasten your gaze on their light.

If you have long held to weeping, never having taken any comfort, now feel joy, forsake bitter tears, and tend to nothing other than rejoicing.

For if it is right that after long labors I am allowed some brief respite, restore my losses with your lasting gaze;

and before the unstable one repents,[65] seek reward for those suffered years, for it seems that Heaven rarely consents to happiness!"

64. See note 42.

65. The reference is to Fortune. The poet depicts the shift from misfortune to happiness upon contemplation of the beloved's light and imagines Fortune to repent her past cruelty. See also poem 45.13.

26

Ombroso colle, amene e verdi piante,
liete piagge profonde e grate valli,
correnti, freschi, e lucidi cristalli,
conforto spesso a le mie pene tante;
segrete selve reverende e sante,
folti boschetti e solitari calli,
soavi fiori persi, bianchi, e gialli,
oppressi da celesti e sacre piante:
a voi, piangendo, già miei duri stenti
narrai più volte; or a voi tutti insieme
voglio parte scoprir de' miei contenti.
Dopo lunghe fatiche e doglie estreme
vidi del mio bel sole i raggi ardenti
quando di veder lor manch'ebbi speme.

Shaded hill, lush, verdant plants, wide, idyllic meadows and serene valleys, fresh-flowing crystalline streams, frequent comfort to my many pains;

secret woods revered and blessed, thick groves and solitary paths, delicate flowers, purple, white, and yellow, walked upon by heavenly sacred feet.

To you in my weeping I often recounted my troubled woes; now to you all together I wish to reveal some of my newfound joys.[66]

After long labors and extreme sorrows[67] I beheld the shining rays of my beautiful sun[68] when I had the least hope of seeing them.[69]

66. The poet in this sonnet evokes the poetic tradition of bucolic elegy, in telling the pastoral landscape of her suffering. A similar scene is imagined in poem 43, with Maria d'Aragona as the figure disclosing her pain to her surroundings as she endures the absence of her husband, Alfonso d'Avalos, away at war. Compare, then, poem 56, where the landscape is imbued with political significance. See note 188.

67. See note 16.

68. See note 42.

69. This poem is a rare instance in Gambara's love poetry in which reunion with the beloved is celebrated.

27

Se più stanno a parir quei duo bei lumi
che pon rasserenar mia vita oscura
e d'ogni oltraggio uman farla sicura
temo ch'anzi 'l suo dì non si consumi.
E pria senz'acqua correran i fiumi,
né avrà più 'l mondo di morte paura,
e la legge del Ciel, che eterna dura,
si romperà, qual nebbia al vento o fumi,
ch'io possa senza lor viver un'ora,
che pur son la mia scorta, e per lor soli
la via di gir al Ciel scorgo ed imparo.
O stella! O fato, del mio mal sì avaro
che 'l mio ben m'allontani, anzi m'involi,
fia mai quel dì ch'io lo riveggia o mora?

If those two beautiful lights[70] that can brighten my dark life and protect it from every mortal offense further delay to appear, I fear my life may burn out before its day.[71]

The rivers will run without water, the world will no longer fear death, and celestial law, which reigns eternal, will dissipate like fog or smoke in the wind

before I can live without them for a moment, for they are my guide, and only because of them I learn and discern the path to Heaven.[72]

Oh star! Oh Fortune, so greedy for my pain that you take away, or rather, steal, my good—will I ever see him again, or shall I die?

70. The eyes of the beloved as a source of radiant light occurs throughout Gambara's love poetry; see notes 14 and 42. The phrase "duo bei lumi" occurs in *Rerum vulgarium fragmenta*, 156, 204, 258, 272, 311. For other instances of "eyes" in Gambara's poetry, see poems 28.1, 29.1 and 30.1.

71. For other instances of the beloved as sun or life-giving force in Gambara's love poetry, see 22.2, 25.3, 26.13, and 27.1–4.

72. Petrarch, *Rerum vulgarium fragmenta*, 13.12–14: "da lei vien l'animosa leggiadra / ch'al ciel ti scorge per destro sentero, / sì ch' i' vo già de la speranza altero" (from her comes the courageous joy that leads you to Heaven along a straight path, so that already I go with high hope).

28[73]

Occhi lucenti e belli:
come esser può ch'in un medesmo instante
nascan da voi sì nove forme e tante?
Lieti, mesti, superbi, umili, alteri
vi mostrate in un punto, onde di speme
e di timor m'empiete,
e tanti effetti dolci, acerbi, e feri
nel cor arso per voi vengono insieme
ad ogn'or che volete.
Or poiché voi mia vita e morte sete,
occhi felici, occhi beati e cari,
siate sempre sereni, allegri, e chiari.

Shining and lovely eyes:[74] how is it that you give birth in an instant to such diverse and wondrous forms?

Happy, sad, proud, humble, scornful, you seem to be all at once, so that you fill me with hope and fear,

and many sweet, bitter, and forceful effects converge in my burnt heart at your will.

Since you are my life and my death, joyous eyes, eyes blessed and dear, may you be always serene, joyful, and bright.

73. Madrigal.

74. See note 70.

29

Dal veder voi, occhi lucenti e chiari,
nasce un piacer ne l'alma, un gaudio tale
ch'ogni sdegno, ogni affanno, ogni gran male
soavi tengo, e chiamo dolci e cari.
Dal non vedervi, poi, lucenti e rari
lumi del viver mio segno fatale,
un sì fiero dolor quest'alma assale
che i giorni miei fa più che assenzio amari.
Quanto contemplo voi sol vivo tanto,
limpide stelle mie soavi e liete;
il resto di mia vita è doglia e pianto;
però se di vedervi ho sì gran sete
maraviglia non è, ch'uom fugge quanto
che può il morire, onde voi schermo sete.

At the sight of you, eyes shining and bright,[75] such joy springs forth in my soul that every dismay, every labor, every great pain I consider gentle and call sweet and dear.

When denied your sight, brilliant rare lights, fatal sign of my living,[76] my soul is beset by a sorrow so fierce that my days are more bitter than absinthe.

I only live as long as I behold you, my clear, lovely, joyous stars; the rest of my life is pain and weeping.

It is no wonder if I have such great thirst to see you, for man flees death however he can, and you are the shield against it.

75. See note 70.

76. The eyes of the beloved serve as a beacon to guide the speaker along the path of life.

30

Vero albergo d'amore, occhi lucenti,
del frale viver mio fermo sostegno:
a voi ricorro ed a voi sempre vegno
per dar qualche riposo a' miei tormenti;
ch'al fulgurar de' vostri raggi ardenti
fugge ogni affano, ogni gravoso sdegno,
e di tal gioia poi resta 'l cor pregno
che loco in me non han pensier dolenti.
Da voi solo procede, occhi beati,
tutto quel ben ch'in questa mortal vita
darmi può 'l Cielo o mia benigna sorte;
siatemi dunque più cortesi e grati,
e col splendor de la beltà infinita
liberate il mio cor d'acerba morte.

True dwelling of love, shining eyes,[77] steadfast support for my frail life: to you I return, and to you I always come, to provide some respite to my torments.

Upon the splendor of your burning rays every trouble, every onerous dismay, flees, and my heart is imbued with such joy that painful thoughts no longer have a place within me.

All the good that Heaven or my benign fate can ever offer me in this mortal life springs forth solely from you, blessed eyes.

May you be even more gracious and kind to me, and with the splendor of your infinite beauty, free my heart from bitter death.

77. See note 70.

POEMS OF PLACE

31

Tu che mostrasti al rozzo mondo prima
mutar le dure ghiande in belle spiche,
e festi sì con l'utili fatiche
che dea ti chiama ogni abitato clima:
e tu, del cui valor canta ogni rima,
primo a insegnare a quelle genti antiche
piantar le viti ne le piagge apriche
per trarne poi liquor di tanta stima:
se con occhi pietosi e mente umile
guarderete ambiduo quel che finora,
vostra dolce mercé, dato n'avete,
di sangue e latte al più fiorito aprile,
con vino e farro i vostri altari ognora
da me onorar con puro cor vedrete.

You[78] who first showed the primitive world how to change hard acorns[79] to beautiful wheat, and thanks to the fruitful labors, every inhabited region calls you goddess:

and you,[80] whom every rhyme honors, first to teach the ancient people to harvest vines on the open slopes and to distill that much praised liquor:

if with merciful eyes and humble minds you each behold the bountiful gifts provided until now by your sweet mercy,

with the blood and the milk[81] of the most fruitful April, and with wine and grain, you will see me honor your blessed altars with the purest heart.

78. The "you" here is Ceres, the Roman goddess of agriculture. See also poem 68.137–144.

79. The image of acorns evokes the literary tradition of the golden age, where one lives in rustic simplicity and pure harmony with the offerings of the land. Another allusion to the golden age in the poem is the evocation of the gods Ceres and Bacchus (see note 80). For other poems alluding to the golden age, see 34 and 68.

80. The second "you" is Bacchus, the Roman god of wine. See also poem 68.137–144.

81. These lines allude to ritual offerings to the gods to ensure a bountiful harvest, which included sacrificing animals and pouring fresh milk or wine on an altar.

32

Onorate acque, e voi, liti beati
ov'il ciel, più tranquillo e più sereno
ch'in altra parte si dimostra, a pieno
sparge i suoi doni a tutti altri negati:
s'i versi miei fosser di stil sì ornati
come di buon voler l'almo ed ameno
vostro sito, di grazie e valor pieno,
farian eterno, e voi cari e pregiati;
ma le mie roche rime e 'l basso ingegno,
troppo inuguali a vostra grande altezza,
non ardiscon, cantando, andar tant'alto,
ch'a ragionar di voi non fora degno
qualsivoglia gran stil pien di dolcezza;
però con l'alma sol v'onoro e esalto.

Honored waters, and you, blessed shores, where Heaven, showing itself here more tranquil and serene than elsewhere, spreads its gifts with bounty while withholding them from all others.[82]

If my verses were as rich in style as they are in good will, this life-giving and pleasant place, full of blessings and honor, they would render eternal, and your shores cherished and prized.

But my coarse rhymes and base wit,[83] far unequal to your greatness, dare not reach such height in song,

since to sing of you any noble style full of sweetness would be unworthy; thus I honor and exalt you only with my soul.

82. The subject of the sonnet may be Correggio or Brescia, though the reference to water in the opening quatrain suggests the subject is more likely Brescia, where the river Mella flows.

83. Gambara frequently presents her poetic efforts with humility, often declaring her ability to be inadequate in representing the greatness of her subject. This may be a self-stylization within the traditional conventions of feminine modesty and virtue, characteristic of the early sixteenth century—especially when we see her employ the trope in poems to well-known literary figures such as Vittoria Colonna, Pietro Aretino, Ludovico Dolce, and Guido Rangone. See poems 34.25–32, 42.12–14, 47.9–11, 50.1–4, and 51.9–11.

33

Poiché, per mia ventura, a veder torno
voi, dolci colli, e voi, chiare e fresch'acque,
e te, cui tanto a la Natura piacque
farti, sito gentil, vago e adorno,
ben posso dire: «Oh fortunato giorno!»
e lodar sempre quel desir che nacque
in me di rivedervi che pria giacque
morto nel cor, di dolor cinto intorno.
Vi veggio or, dunque, e tal dolcezza sento
che quante mai da la Fortuna offese
ricevute ho sinor pongo in oblio;
così sempre vi sia largo e cortese,
lochi beati, il Ciel, come in me spento
è, se non di voi soli, ogni desio.

Since I have the fortune to return to see you,[84] sweet hills, and you, limpid and fresh springs,[85] and you, noble place that Nature was so eager to make pleasing and ornate,

then I can say: "Oh blessed day!" and forever praise the desire born in me to see you again that once lay lifeless in my heart, enshrouded by heavy pain.[86]

I see you now, and the sweetness I feel is such that I cast aside into oblivion any offenses Fortune ever gave me.

May Heaven be always as generous and gracious to you, blessed places:[87] for extinct in me is every desire, other than the desire for you.

84. Given, again, the emphasis on the water of the region, this is likely a poem about Brescia. Gambara included this poem in a letter to Pietro Bembo dated January 20, 1533, the period of the Gambara family's return to Brescia, the waters referred to being the river Mella.

85. Petrarch, *Rerum vulgarium fragmenta*, 126.1: "Chiare fresche et dolci acque" (Clear, fresh, sweet waters).

86. The pain felt while she is away from Brescia recalls the pain felt in absence of the beloved. Poem 34 likens the joy felt in the return to Brescia to that felt by two reunited lovers.

87. The phrase "lochi beati"—possibly a self-referential play on the "occhi beati" of Gambara's love poetry—is used in another poem that celebrates Brescia, see 34.25.

34[88]

Con quel caldo desio che nascer sole
in petto di chi torna, amando, assente,
gli occhi vaghi a vedere e le parole
dolci a scoltar del suo bel foco ardente;
con quel proprio voi, piagge al mondo sole,
fresch'acque, ombrosi colli, e te, possente
più d'altra che 'l sol miri andando intorno,
bella e lieta cittade, a veder torno.

Salve, mia bella patria, o tu, felice
tanto amato dal Ciel ricco paese,
ch'a guisa di leggiadra alma fenice
mostri l'alto valor chiaro e palese;
Natura, a te sol madre e pia nutrice,
ha fatto agli altri mille gravi offese
spogliandogli di quanto avean di buono
per farne a te cortese e largo dono.

Non tigri, non leoni, e non serpenti
nascono in te, nemici a l'uman seme,
non erbe venenose, a dar possenti
l'acerba morte allor che men si teme,
ma fiere isnelle e ben pasciuti armenti
scherzar si veggion per i campi insieme
pieni d'erbe gentili e vaghi fiori
spargendo grazïosi e cari odori.

Ma perché a dir di voi, lochi beati,
ogn'alto stile saria roco e basso
il carco d'onorarvi a più pregiati
sublimi ingegni e glorïosi lasso;
da me sarete col pensier lodati,
e con l'anima sempre e ad ogni passo,
con la memoria vostra in mezzo il core,
quanto fia 'l mio potere, farovvi onore.[89]

88. Composed in ottava rima.

89. The line reads "presto fia 'l mio potere in farvi onore" per Bullock; amended here to "quanto fia 'l mio potere, farovvi onore" following Rizzardi (Gambara, *Rime e lettere di Veronica Gambara*, 22).

With that warm desire oftimes born in the heart of one who returns having loved in absence to see the limpid eyes and hear the sweet words of his beautiful burning flame;[90] so I return to see you, peerless shores, fresh waters, shaded hills, and you, beautiful and joyful city, more powerful than any other the sun can see in its turning.

Greetings, my beautiful homeland,[91] and salutations to you, rich country, so happy and beloved by the heavens, radiating your clear and illustrious valor as a noble and graceful phoenix.[92] Nature, mother and kind nurse only to you, imposed thousands of grave offenses upon other lands, divesting them of any bounty they had in order to give gracious and abundant gifts to you.

No tigers, lions, nor serpents—enemies of the human race—are born from you, nor are poisonous herbs, powerful in giving bitter death when one fears it least; instead, swift beasts and strong herds roam together across the fields full of lush grass and beautiful flowers spreading pleasant, sweet perfumes.[93]

Because every noble style would be too coarse and low to sing of you,[94] blessed places,[95] I leave the duty of honoring you to more esteemed and celebrated minds. I will always praise you in my thoughts and in my soul, and with each step I take, with the memory of you nestled in my heart, as much as I can I will honor you.

90. The joy of returning to Brescia is like that felt by two lovers reunited after a long absence. See poem 33.

91. The subject is Brescia, the homeland of the Gambara family. The waters referred to are those of the river Mella.

92. The reference to the myth of the phoenix—the firebird that arose out of its own ashes from death to life again—represents the return of political stability to the Brescia region and the reinstatement of Gambara rule to its feudal territory after a period of exile that began in 1516, a restoration brought about by Charles V in 1529. The renewed political strength of Brescia is emphasized throughout the poem.

93. Her family's territory is depicted as an idyllic pastoral landscape of the golden age. For other meditations on the golden age in Gambara's poetry, see poems 31 and 68.

94. See note 83.

95. See note 87.

POEMS OF CORRESPONDENCE AND *ENCOMIA*

35

Non t'ammirar, s'a te, non visto mai,
ardisco di mandar queste mie carte,
ché tue virtù, per tutto 'l mondo sparte,
mi fan far quel ch'ancor non feci mai.
E so che tal ardir non biasmerai
se quelle ben misuri a parte a parte;
lor fan ch'a forza è ognun constretto amarte,
però per questo me excusata arrai.
Quelle m'han spinta a far ch'io ti palesi
quant'io t'amo ed onoro, e quanto ancora
miei spiriti omai sian di servirti accesi;
e l'alta umanità, che 'n te dimora,
mi porse ardir assai più che non cresi
di far quel ch'ho tardato infin ad ora.

Do not be surprised if, though I have never seen you,[96] I dare to send you these writings of mine,[97] since your virtues,[98] known throughout the world, made me do what I have never done before.

I know that you will not blame my boldness,[99] if only you consider your virtues one by one; they compel everyone to love you, and for this reason you will pardon me.

They impelled me to reveal how greatly I love and admire you, and how my spirits are inflamed by the desire to serve you;

the great benevolence that resides within you gave me the courage, more than I ever imagined, to do that which I had delayed until now.

96. This poem is Gambara's first known sonnet to Pietro Bembo (1470–1547), composed sometime in the year 1504. See Gambara, *Le rime*, 72.

97. As the poem points out, this is the first time Gambara has shared her writing with Bembo; see also the next line and the final terzina.

98. While the sonnet sets out to introduce Gambara's poetry to Bembo, the subject of the poem is the virtue of her recipient. Bembo's virtues are the operating force in the poem because they inspire and impel the poet to action.

99. Gambara's humility is characteristic of the conventions of feminine modesty and virtue of the early sixteenth century. It also serves to cast the elder male Bembo in the role of mentor to the young female Gambara as she seeks to fulfill aspirations of literary fame.

36

A l'ardente desio ch'ognor m'accende
di seguir nel camin ch'al Ciel conduce
sol voi mancava, o mia serena luce,
per discacciar la nebbia che m'offende.
Or, poiché 'l vostro raggio in me risplende,
per quella strada ch'a ben far ne induce
vengo dietro di voi, fidato duce,
che 'l mio voler più oltra non si stende.
Bassi pensieri in me non han più loco;
ogni vil voglia è spenta, e sol d'onore
e di rara virtù l'alma si pasce,
dolce mio caro ed onorato foco,
poscia che dal gentil vostro calore
eterna fama e vera gloria nasce.

The burning desire that ever inspires me to follow the path that leads to Heaven lacked only you,[100] my serene light, to chase away the mist that obscured my way.[101]

Now that your ray shines within me, I follow you as my faithful guide along the path that leads to goodness, and my desire extends no further.

Base thoughts no longer reside in me, every vile desire is extinguished, and my soul feeds solely on honor and exceptional virtue,[102]

my sweet, dear, and honored flame, because from your noble warmth, eternal fame and true glory are born.[103]

100. Pietro Bembo, this poem was sent to him in 1529. See Gambara, *Le rime*, 95–96.

101. The reference to Bembo as the "serene light" that leads the poet to heaven is a gender inversion of the relation of Laura to Petrarch, where the female Laura is cast as the guide to heaven whom the male Petrarch seeks to follow. See Petrarch, *Rerum vulgarium fragmenta*, 13.12–14: "da lei vien l'animosa leggiadra / ch'al ciel ti scorge per destro sentero, / sì ch' i' vo già de la speranza altero" (from her comes the courageous joy that leads you to Heaven along a straight path, so that already I go high with hope). The guidance that Bembo provides Gambara is moral in its essence.

102. Gambara would have benefited from fashioning herself as an icon of virtue in her role as a ruling widow regent. Her hold on her seat of power—to which she was connected by marriage, not by birth—could have been endangered if she were suspected of unchaste relations. For other instances of the poet's self-fashioning as a woman of exemplary virtue, see poems 41.9–14 and 68.209–16.

103. See note 101.

37

Quella donna gentil, ch'amaste tanto
mentre fu 'n terra, or nel Cïelo sciolta
dal grave incarco vive, ed indi ascolta
i sospir vostri e l'angoscioso pianto.
Di voi si duole e così dice: «Ahi, quanto
con la tua vita, solo a pianger volta,
turbi 'l mio stato e la mia pace molta,
e questo viver mio felice e santo!
Io non t'amai perché 'l mio bene odiassi,
né in man ti dei de la mia vita 'l freno
perch'il frale di me solo pregiassi;
dunque asciuga le lagrime che 'l seno
ti bagnan sempre, e l'alma, che 'n Ciel stassi,
ama più che non festi il suo terreno!»

That noble lady,[104] whom you dearly loved while she resided on earth, now lives in Heaven, free from our heavy burden,[105] and from there she listens to your heavy sighs and anguished tears.

She complains of you and says:[106] "Alas! With your life devoted only to weeping, how you disturb my state, my abundant peace, and this life of mine, so joyful and blessed!

104. The sonnet was composed for Pietro Bembo upon the death of his companion, Ambrogina Faustina Morosina della Torre, in 1535. See Gambara, *Le rime*, 116–17.

105. The "burden" refers to the burden of mortal life on earth, as opposed to the liberation of eternal life in Paradise. See also poem 39.3.

106. When Gambara marked her return to public circulation of her poetry with the sonnet composed for Pietro Bembo in 1529 (see poem 36), she no longer composed poems from the point of view of a first-person poet-persona in love. This thematic shift may be understood to result from her political position as the governing dowager Countess of Correggio; she stood to benefit from a different kind of public persona, one imbued with virtue, who spends the years of her widowhood in devout chastity. This is not to say that the theme of love disappears from her mature verse altogether. Gambara composed sonnets in honor of loving relationships, such as those of Pietro Bembo and Morosina, Pietro Aretino and Angela Tornimbeni, and Alfonso d'Avalos and Maria d'Aragona. In these poems, Gambara frequently speaks in the voice of the woman in the relationship to center on the female perspective. For other instances in which Gambara adopts the voice of the female beloved speaking to the male recipient of her sonnet, see poems 43.5–11 and 44.6–14.

I did not love you for you to spurn my good, nor did I hand you the reins of my life for you to love only the frail part of me.[107]

So dry the tears that endlessly bathe your chest, and love my soul as it resides in Heaven more than you loved its form on earth!"[108]

107. The "frail part" is the mortal body.

108. To console Bembo in his grief upon the death of Morosina, Gambara is alluding to Bembo's Neoplatonic philosophy, in which the body is the earthly counterpart to the soul in heaven and the soul is to be loved more than the body. See also poem 6.12–14.

38

Or che sei ritornata, alma felice,
al Ciel, onde partisti, e lieta miri
le superne bellezze, e 'n dolci giri
scorgi ciò che a mortal occhi non lice,
porgi l'orecchie al suon triste e 'nfelice
de le lagrime nostre e dei sospiri;
poi dolerti di noi pietà t'inspiri
se del nostro dolor sei la radice.
Rimaso è al tuo partir il mondo oscuro,
di tenebre vestito, e senza onore
le Muse e Apollo, e i spirti illustri e chiari,
che sotto l'ombra tua quà per sicuro
camin givan cantando, or pien di amari
e dogliosi pensier passano l'ore.

Now that you[109] have returned, happy soul,[110] to Heaven, whence you came, and joyfully gaze at the celestial beauties, and in sweet circles[111] behold visions denied to mortal sight,

listen to the sad, unhappy sound of our tears and sighs; may such sorrow inspire your pity for us, for you are the root of our pain.

The world darkened upon your departure, cloaked in shadows; the Muses[112] and Apollo[113] were deprived of honor; and all the illustrious and bright spirits,

who in the past could sing along a safe path beneath your protective shade, now spend their days with bitter and mournful thoughts.[114]

109. The sonnet is a eulogy upon the death of Pietro Bembo in 1547. See Gambara, *Le rime*, 164.

110. See Petrarch, *Rerum vulgarium fragmenta*, 282.1: "Alma felice che soventi torni" (Happy soul who often comes back).

111. The reference is to the heavenly circles of Paradise.

112. The Muses in Greek mythology inspire artistic production; the reference underscores Bembo's influence in the literary arts.

113. Apollo, patron god of poetry in the Greek and Roman traditions; the allusion underscores Bembo's role as a poet.

114. The group of mourners imagined here are poets who, on Bembo's death, have lost their literary model.

39

Riser gli spirti angelici e celesti
e più luce mostrò ciascuna stella
quando dal grave incarco, anima bella,
sciolta dinanzi al tuo Fattor giungesti,
e, tutta umile: «Ecco, Signor» dicesti,
«la tua devota ubedïente ancella
Ti rende, al Tuo voler non mai rubella,
doppi i talenti Tuoi che già le desti!»
Ed Ei rispose: «O mia fedele e cara:
entra a goder il mio beato Regno,
anzi che 'l mondo fosse a te promesso!»
Tal ebbe fin la glorïosa e chiara
tua vita, o Bembo, e sì, come eri degno,
ti fu pregio immortal là su concesso.

The angelic and celestial spirits smiled and every star beamed more light when you, beautiful soul,[115] freed from the heavy burden,[116] appeared before your Creator,

and humbly said, "Here, Lord, Your devoted and obedient servant, never rebellious to Your will, returns double the talents that You gave him!"[117]

The Lord replied, "My dear, faithful one: enter and enjoy my blessed Kingdom, already promised to you before the world existed!"[118]

Such was the end of your glorious and famous life, dear Bembo, and as you deserved, an immortal prize was given to you above.

115. The sonnet is a eulogy for Pietro Bembo (d. 1547). See Gambara, *Le rime*, 165.

116. See note 105.

117. The reference is to the parable of the talents in Matthew 25:14–30, to illustrate the ability of Bembo's soul to multiply in virtue.

118. This line suggests that Gambara was exploring ideas of predestination, which may be rooted in the Reformation doctrine of *sola fide*, that God selects those he wishes to save through his love, a choice that humans are unable to control or alter by their deeds. Bembo's salvation was long ordained by God, and not a result of the good works referred to in the poem. For another sonnet that explores these ideas, see poem 66.

40

Altri boschi, altri prati, ed altri monti,
felice e lieto Bardo, or godi e miri,
ed altre ninfe vedi, in vaghi giri
danzar cantando intorno a fresche fonti,
e ad altri ch'a mortali ora racconti
i moderati tuoi santi desiri,
né più fuor del tuo petto escon sospiri,
di dolor segni manifesti e conti,
ma, beato nel Ciel, nascer l'aurora
e sotto i piedi tuoi vedi le stelle
produr girando i vari effetti suoi,
e vedi che i pastor d'erbe novelle
sacrificio ti fanno, e dicon poi:
«Sii propizio a chi t'ama e a chi t'onora!»

Other forests, other meadows, and other mountains you now behold and enjoy, happy, serene Bardo,[119] and you see other nymphs singing in joyful circles around fresh springs;

to other than mortals you recount your chaste and saintly desires; and sighs—clear signs of pain[120]—no longer emanate from your chest.

Instead, blissful in Heaven, you now see the birth of dawn and the stars beneath your feet, generating their effects with their turning;

and you see shepherds sacrifice fresh branches to you as they say, "May you be gracious to those who love and honor you!"

119. The person addressed in this poem is unknown.

120. In reference to mortal life.

41[121]

Mentre da vaghi e giovenil penseri
fui nutrita, or temendo ora sperando,
piangendo or trista ed or lieta cantando,
da desir combattuta or falsi or veri,
con accenti sfogai pietosi e fieri
i concetti del cor, che, spesso amando
il suo mal assai più che 'l ben cercando,
consumava doglioso i giorni intieri.
Or, che d'altri pensieri e d'altre voglie
pasco la mente, a le già care rime
ho posto ed a lo stil silenzio eterno,
e se, allor vaneggiando, a quelle prime
sciocchezze intesi, ora il pentirmi toglie,
la colpa palesando, il duol interno.

While I was nourished by wandering and youthful thoughts, now fearing, now hoping, now crying in pain, now singing in delight, grappling with both false and true desires,

with fierce and pitiful tones I vented the affairs of my heart, which, seeking its own pain over well-being, spent entire days in agony.[122]

Now that my mind feeds on different thoughts and desires,[123] I have placed my once dear rhymes and style in eternal silence;[124]

and if then in my nonsense I devoted myself to those youthful follies, now my repentance,[125] by revealing my guilt, relieves the inner pain.

121. Vittoria Colonna (1490–1547) is the recipient of this sonnet, composed in 1532. See Gambara, *Le rime*, 102–3.

122. Gambara's reflection on the love poetry that dominated her early work recalls the prefatory sonnet of Petrarch's *Rerum vulgarium fragmenta*, especially the lines "quei sospiri ond'io nudriva 'l core" (those sighs with which I nourished my heart) and "del vario stile in ch'io piango et ragiono / fra le vane speranze e 'l van dolore" (for the varied style in which I weep and speak between vain hopes and vain sorrow).

123. See note 102.

124. Gambara is marking a thematic shift in her poetry away from the love poems composed at the start of her poetic career. See note 106.

125. The repentance of the poet echoes that of Petrarch, *Rerum vulgarium fragmenta*, 1.12–14: "e del mio vaneggiar vergogna è 'l frutto, / e 'l pentersi, e 'l conoscer

42

O de la nostra etade unica gloria,
donna saggia, leggiadra, anzi divina,
a la qual reverente oggi s'inchina
chiunque è degno di famosa istoria:
ben fia eterna di voi qua giù memoria,
né potrà il tempo con la sua ruina
far del bel nome vostro empia rapina,
ma di lui porterete alma vittoria.
Il sesso nostro un sacro e nobil tempio
dovria, come già a Palla e a Febo, farvi,
di ricchi marmi e di finissim'oro,
e, poiché di virtù sete l'esempio,
vorrei, Donna, poter tanto lodarvi
quanto vi riverisco, amo, ed adoro.

Oh sole glory of our age, wise, graceful, or better still, divine woman,[126] to whom all that are worthy of fame in history bow down in reverence;

the memory of you on earth will be eternal, nor will Time with its destructive power be able to relegate your noble name to oblivion, for over Time you will achieve splendid victory.[127]

Our sex should build you a sacred and noble temple, as was the custom for Pallas[128] and Phoebus,[129] made of the richest marbles and the finest gold.[130]

---

chiaramente / che quanto piace al mondo è breve sogno" (and of my raving, shame is the fruit, and repentance, and the clear knowledge that whatever pleases in the world is but a brief dream).

126. Vittoria Colonna is the dedicatee of this sonnet. See Gambara, *Le rime*, 103–4.

127. The Italian word "vittoria" is a Petrarchan wordplay on Colonna's first name, Vittoria, meaning victory.

128. Pallas Athena, patron of wisdom in this context. In this poem, Colonna is praised for her intellect and wisdom, which are equal to those of the gods and therefore deserving of an honorary monument.

129. Phoebus Apollo, god of poetry in Greek and Roman traditions.

130. Gambara employs similar ekphrasis in depicting an imagined monument in honor of Charles V in poem 56.

Being the true example of virtue as you are, dear Lady, I wish only that I were able to praise you as much as I revere, love, and adore you.[131]

131. See note 83.

43[132]

Là dove or d'erbe adorna ambe le sponde
il bel Sebeto, e le campagne infiora,
Amarilli gentil, che v'ama e adora,
tal spesso dice, al mormorar de l'onde:
«Deh! perché, lassa! agli occhi miei s'asconde
l'altero sguardo ch'oggi 'l mondo onora?
E perché 'l fier desio, che m'innamora,
cresce coi fiori e con le nove fronde?
E 'l mio Davalo, forse intento sempre
con l'armi e con l'ingegno a render vano
il nemico furor, di me non cura?»
Così, piena d'amor e di paura,
la bella donna in disusate tempre
si strugge del star vostro a lei lontano.

Where the beautiful Sebeto[133] decorates both banks with herbs and fills the fields with flowers, the noble Amaryllis,[134] who loves and adores you, often says amid the murmuring currents:[135]

"Alas! Why does that proud glance, now honored by the whole world, hide from my sight?[136] Why does the fierce desire that enamors me grow stronger with the blossom of new flowers and branches?[137]

132. This sonnet was composed for Maria d'Aragona (1503–68) and Alfonso d'Avalos (1502–46). See Gambara, *Le rime*, 91–92.

133. The river Sebeto flows to the east of Naples, in the region where the d'Avalos family resided. See also poem 44.2.

134. Maria d'Aragona. Gambara refers to d'Aragona using a pastoral name from Virgil's *Bucolics*, *Eclogue* 1; the name Amaryllis imbues the poem with the tones and associations of the pastoral tradition.

135. Poem 26 also has a woman addressing her lament for the absence of the beloved to the landscape. Although Gambara here recalls themes and images from her love poetry (pain felt in absence of the beloved, the renewal of love in springtime), she here writes not of herself as the poet-persona, but of the trials of another woman. See notes 66 and 106.

136. Gambara is referring to Alfonso d'Avalos, distant from d'Aragona because of his service in the imperial army of Charles V, likely between the years 1543 and1544.

137. See note 38.

Maybe my d'Avalos, always intent to defeat the enemy frenzy with the force of arms and intellect,[138] does not care about me?"

Thus, full of love and fear, the beautiful woman in unaccustomed ways laments your distance.

138. In reference to d'Avalos's role as a military general who fought in battle and devised military strategy.

44[139]

Se lungi dagli amati e cari lumi
de la bella Amarilli in doglia e 'n pianto,
Signor, sempre vivete, ella altrettanto
sparge per voi dagli occhi amari fiumi,
e ciò che mira le par ombre e fumi
oscuri ed atre, e spesso dice: «Ahi! Quanto
offendi 'l nostro amor pudico e santo
e 'l viver mio col tuo dolor consumi!
Non basta ben che per mia doglia eterna
anzi tempo di vita ha il Cielo avaro
tolto il mio dopo te sommo diletto?
Però se m'ami, e se mia doglia interna
cerchi addolcir, pon freno al duolo amaro,
che da te solo ogni conforto aspetto».

If far from the dear and beloved eyes of beautiful Amaryllis,[140] you, lord,[141] live constantly in grief and sorrow, she too cries rivers of tears for you,

and everything in her sight appears as shadows and dark smoke, and often she says,[142] "Alas! How you offend our chaste, saintly love, and consume my life with your pain!

Is it not enough that, for my eternal anguish, selfish Heaven stole before his time my highest pleasure, second only to you?[143]

Thus, if you love me and want to sweeten my inner grief, restrain your bitter pain, since I await comfort only from you."

139. This sonnet was composed for Maria d'Aragona and Alfonso d'Avalos. See Gambara, *Le rime*, 92–93.

140. Maria d'Aragona. See note 134.

141. Alfonso d'Avalos. See note 136.

142. See note 106.

143. This likely refers to the death of another member of Maria d'Aragona's family, possibly Ferrante d'Avalos, the husband of Vittoria Colonna, but the intimacy of the lament suggests otherwise.

45[144]

Donna gentil, che così largamente
de le doti del Ciel foste arricchita,
che per mostrar la forza sua infinita
fece voi così rara ed excellente:
fuggan da vostra altera e real mente
tutti i pensier ch'a darvi oscura vita
fosser bastanti, perché omai finita
è la guerra di lui troppo possente.
E se finor con mille oltraggi ed onte
v'ha mostrato Fortuna il fiero volto
stato è sol per provar l'alto valore
che 'n voi soggiorna; or la serena fronte
vi volge, e, del suo error pentita molto,
quanto fu il mal tanto fia il ben maggiore.

Noble lady,[145] so enriched with gifts from Heaven, which to display its infinite powers made you truly exceptional and unique:

may all the thoughts that could be enough to cast darkness over your life vanish from your noble and regal mind, for now the war of him, so forceful, is over.[146]

If until now with thousands of insults and abuses, Fortune has shown you only her cruel face, it was only to test the great virtue

that resides within you. Now she shows you her serene face, having repented her error,[147] so may your pleasure be greater than any pain once endured.

144. This sonnet was composed for Maria d'Aragona and Alfonso d'Avalos. See Gambara, *Le rime*, 93–94.

145. Maria d'Aragona.

146. The "guerra di lui" (war of him) is a play on the emotional war experienced by d'Aragona in her husband's absence, and the literal war d'Avalos was fighting. Thus, the return of d'Avalos marks the end of both struggles.

147. See note 65.

46

Ben si può dir che a voi largo e cortese,
bella donna, sia stato il Cielo avaro
de le sue grazie poiché 'l spirto chiaro
per voi de l'Arretino arse e si accese;
questo[148] saran gli schermi e le diffese
che vi toranno al morso empio ed amaro
del fiero tempo, e questo fia 'l riparo
contra le gravi sue pungenti offese.
Certo giusta cagion di gire altera
più ch'altra avete, poiché sol vi onora
quello che tutto il mondo onora e teme;
quanti diranno, ragionando ancora,
«Sol con Beatrice fia e con Laura insieme,
Sirena eterna ne la terza spera!»

One may well say that Heaven, which often withholds its graces, was generous and kind to you, beautiful lady,[149] because the bright spirit of Aretino[150] caught fire and burned for love of you;

this will be your protection and defense against the bitter and merciless jaws of cruel Time; this will be the shield against its harsh, piercing attacks.

You have good reason to walk more proudly than any other woman, because he, whom the whole world fears, honors you.[151]

Thus how many will say, "Only with Beatrice and Laura will Sirena share eternal life in the third sphere!"[152]

148. "Queste" per Bullock; amended to "questo" following the manuscript in Venice's Marciana Library. See Gambara, *Le rime*, 114.

149. Angela Tornimbeni, the beloved of Pietro Aretino and wife of Gian Antonio Sirena.

150. Pietro Aretino (1492–1556) is the recipient of this sonnet. See Gambara, *Le rime*, 114–16.

151. Gambara is making a subtle reference to the notoriety Aretino earned through his satirical writing, which led Ariosto to call him the *flagello dei principi* (scourge of princes).

152. Gambara imagines an alignment of the iconic female beloveds of Italian letters (Dante's Beatrice and Petrarch's Laura) with Aretino's Angela. Here she imagines the three women united together in Paradise.

47

Voi, che fra l'altre doti e pregi vostri
bagnaste al dotto fonte i labbri santi,
con vostra pace quanti oltraggi e quanti
fate a le Muse, a voi, ai tempi nostri
poiché non date, con vostri alti inchiostri,
lume ai tardi intelletti, ch'ora erranti
se ne van ciechi senza guida inanti
che la chiara e la dritta via lor mostri!
Io per me non mi levo tanto in alto,
e, come fa tra pochi quell'amico,
non mi presumo invano, e non mi esalto.
Voglion le Muse l'ozio e il tempo aprico;
a me Fortuna è dura più che smalto;
il verno mi combatte, e il mar nemico.

You,[153] who among your other gifts and merits wetted your saintly lips in the learned spring, if I may tell the truth, how you offend the Muses,[154] yourself, and our times,

because with your noble inks you do not offer light to lesser minds, who now wander blind without a guide ahead to show them the true and straight path.

I myself do not rise to such heights, and, like that one friend among a few,[155] I do not boast vainly, nor do I indulge in self-praise.[156]

The Muses require leisure and pleasant times; to me Fortune is harder than enamel, the winter battles against me, and the sea is my enemy.[157]

153. Pietro Aretino is the recipient of this sonnet. See Gambara, *Le rime*, 118.

154. The muses in Greek mythology inspire artistic production; the reference here alludes to Aretino's influence in the literary arts. However, the sonnet laments the fact that Aretino does not draw on his talent to serve as a mentor to writers—a role Gambara highly praises in her poetry on Pietro Bembo in poems 35, 36, and 38.

155. It is not clear to whom Gambara is referring, though the indication is that she shared acquaintances with Aretino within the literary community.

156. See note 83.

157. Gambara is likely referring to her political responsibilities as the governing dowager Countess of Correggio.

48

Cognoscendo, Signor, cosa più grata
non esserti che aver viva colei
che più che te stesso ami ed amar dei,
per esser di bellezze unica nata,
ma non potendo aver tal cosa amata,
com'io pel ben d'ambi voi duo vorrei,
penso che, se non viva aver poi lei,
caro ti fia che in carta a te sia data.
Così non sapendo io ch'altro don farte
più degno ed excellente che di quella
che tanto ami, Signor, l'effigie darte,
onde la mando, non come lei bella,
perché se insieme fosse ogni umana arte
dal ver non potria far sì chiara stella.

I know, dear Sir,[158] that nothing would be more precious to you than to have in life the one you love more than yourself, as you should, since she was born of unique beauty.

Yet unable to have your beloved, as I would wish for the good of you both, I think that if you cannot have her in life you would be grateful to have her on paper.

Therefore, not knowing any other gift to give you more worthy and exceptional than the portrait of the one you love so much, Sir,

I send it to you, though it is not as beautiful as she, for even if every human art came together, it could not reproduce such a bright star.

158. The recipient of this sonnet is unknown.

49

Molza: se ben dal vago aer sereno
lontano sete, e da le piagge apriche
di Roma, tanto a' pensier vostri amiche
che senza par che 'l cor vi venga meno,
non vogliate però chiudere il seno
a le dolcezze de la patria antiche,
sicuro porto alfin de le fatiche
vostre sì gravi e di riposo pieno.
La moglie, i figli, i dolci amici cari
lieto godete, e col gioir di loro
temprate il duol, se pur dentro vi preme;
ed io, che i doni a voi celesti e rari
dal Ciel concessi e 'l vostro nome adoro,
prego che me con gli altri amiate insieme.

Molza,[159] although you are distant from the beautiful, serene air and the bright shores of Rome,[160] so dear to your thoughts that in their absence your heart seems to weaken,

do not close your heart to the ancient sweetness of your fatherland—secure haven for you to rest at the end of your heavy labors.

Enjoy the company of your wife, your children, and your dearly beloved friends; temper your pain, if you have any, with the pleasure of their company;

and I, who adore your name and the rare gifts granted to you from Heaven, pray you also love me alongside them.

159. Francesco Maria Molza (1489–1544), poet and courtier to Ippolito de' Medici.

160. The sonnet consoles Molza in his longing to return to Rome.

50

Se tardo a dir di voi, Dolce gentile,
è stato il rozzo mio debile ingegno;
fu la cagion perché cognosce indegno
a tal soggetto ogni onorato stile;
che se questo non era esca e focile
non accendono foco in secco legno
sì tosto come avrei tolto per segno
voi del mio dir, benché in suon basso, umile.
Ma le vostre leggiadre e dolci rime
mi spaventar sì ch'io non ebbi ardire
di rispondervi allor con carta e 'nchiostro;
pur dirò questo sol, senza più dire:
che non sì saldo in bel marmo s'imprime
come saldo nel core ho il valor vostro.

If I am late in writing of you, kind Dolce,[161] it is due only to my coarse and weak talent, knowing that every honored style is inadequate to such a subject;[162]

had it not been for this reason, tinder and flint could not light a fire with dry wood as fast as I would have made you the subject of my writing, though in base and humble style.

Your sweet and graceful rhymes astounded me so that I did not dare to reply to you with paper and ink;

thus I will add only this, and say no more: one could not engrave in the finest marble as firmly as I hold your virtue in my heart.

161. Ludovico Dolce (1508?–68), well-known writer and prominent figure in the Venetian printing industry.

162. See note 83.

51

Pentito forse il Ciel, fiero nemico
di questa grave mia noiosa vita,
mercé de la virtù vostra infinita,
cangiate voglie or mi si mostra amico;
l'alto vostro valor, pari a l'antico,
vostre rime leggiadre, alma gradita,
tal forza han data a la virtù smarrita
che di dolci pensier or mi nutrico.
Duolmi sol ch'io non sia, sappian gli dei,
quale il mio gran Rangon ha detto e dice,
degno ben lui di più di mille Orfei;
ma, lodandomi voi, qual la fenice,
ricca di eterno onor volando andrei
sopra quante fur mai lieta e felice.

Perhaps Heaven, fierce enemy to my heavy and noisome life, having repented, has transformed its desires and is now friendly toward me, thanks to your infinite virtue.

Your noble worthiness—equal to that of the ancients—and your elegant rhymes, beloved soul, have given such strength to my lost virtue that now I feed on sweet thoughts.

I am only sorry that I am not equal to what my great Rangon[163]—who merits more than a thousand Orpheuses[164]—says of me,[165] as the gods well know.

But if you were to praise me, I would go flying like a phoenix, happy and joyful and full of eternal honor, over all who have ever existed.

163. Guido Rangone (1485–1539), a famous *condottiere* who fought for the Bentivoglio family of Bologna, for the Republic of Venice, and for Pope Leo X.

164. Orpheus, the great poet and musician of ancient Greek myth, whose songs could tame wild beasts and move stones.

165. See note 83.

POLITICAL POEMS

52

Guida con la man forte al camin dritto,
Signor, le genti Tue ch'armate vanno
per dar a' Tuoi nemici acerbo danno
e per Tua gloria a far Cesare invitto.
Quell'ira e quel furor, che già in Egitto
mostrasti, adopra or contra quei che stanno
duri per colmar noi d'eterno affanno,
qual Faraone il Tuo Israele afflitto.
Mira con pietoso occhio e vedrai quanto,
per racquistar la già perduta gregge,
s'affliga ed usi ogni arte il Pastor santo;
fa che si vegga che 'l favor Tuo regge
quest'alta impresa, alfin cagion di tanto
utile e onor a la cristiana legge.

Lord, guide with a strong hand toward the right path Your people who charge forward in arms, to bring bitter harm upon Your enemies[166] and, in the name of Your glory, to keep Caesar[167] unvanquished.

Now exert the same rage and fury that You once showed in Egypt against those determined to assail us with infinite harm, like a new Pharaoh against Your afflicted Israel.[168]

166. The poem addresses the war between Charles V's imperial army and the Ottoman Empire under Suleiman the Magnificent, specifically the emperor's successful military campaign in Tunis against the Turkish navy, commanded by the admiral Hayreddin Barbarossa, in 1535. For further references to this campaign and Barbarossa's defeat, see poems 53, 54.9–11, 56.12–14, 57.12–14; see also note 180.

167. In referring to Charles V as "Caesar," Gambara places Charles in the imperial line descended from Julius Caesar. This imagery was a part of Charles V's imperial conceit, and it was especially significant in the campaign for his dominance over the Mediterranean against the Ottoman Empire. For other instances in which Gambara associates Charles V with the Caesars, see poems 55, 56.10–11, and 57.4–12.

168. Gambara is referring to the punishments imposed by God on the Egyptians when they held the Israelites in captivity; see Exodus 7–12.

Look with a merciful eye and You will see how the saintly Shepherd toils and uses every art to recover the once lost flock;[169]

let the world see that Your will supports the noble enterprise that will ultimately bring great benefit and honor to the Christian faith.[170]

169. The reference is to John 10:11–16, when Jesus proclaims he is the good shepherd who will bring together all sheep, including those lost or scattered. Gambara uses the metaphor of the "pastor santo" and "perduta gregge" to describe Alessandro Farnese, Pope Paul III (1534–49). Such imagery occurs throughout Gambara's political poems; see 59.9–11, 60.4, 61.9–11, and 62.10.

170. Gambara casts the war between Charles V and the Ottoman Empire as a Christian crusade against Islam. This imagery implies that Charles V is intent on reviving the religious charge of the imperial office.

53

Cantin le ninfe co' soavi accenti,
e 'l tuo Proteo, Nettuno, e tuoi Tritoni
facciano a l'armonia de' dolci suoni
star l'onde, e i pesci ad ascoltar intenti.
E tu, che reggi e sol comandi a' venti,
quelli che fanno le tempeste e i tuoni
legati serba, e uscir de le prigioni
chi fa tranquillo il mar lieto consenti
acciò che senza danno e vada e torni
questo non fabuloso o finto Giove,
del secolo infelice unica speme.
Dal divino saper tal grazia piove
che sol può far felici i nostri giorni,
e salvo lui fia il mondo salvo insieme.

May the nymphs sing with gentle accents, and may your Proteus,[171] Neptune,[172] and your Tritons[173] quiet the waves and still the fish to listen to the harmony of sweet sounds.

And you,[174] who alone rule and command over the winds, keep tied those that cause tempests and thunders, and release with joy those that render the sea tranquil,

so that this neither false nor fictitious Jove[175]—the sole hope for our unhappy times—may depart and return without harm.[176]

Such a powerful grace, which alone can make our days happy, rains down from divine wisdom, and if he is safe, the world will be safe with him.

171. Proteus, sea god of Greek mythology.

172. Neptune, sea god of Roman mythology.

173. Tritons are minor divinities of the sea; the name is derived from that of the Greek god Triton, messenger of the sea.

174. Zephyrus, Greek god of the west wind.

175. Another name for Jupiter, the patron god of Rome.

176. The poem bids the fleet of Charles V a safe voyage in the expedition to Tunis to battle the Ottoman Empire's fleet in 1535. See poem 52.

54

Mira 'l gran Carlo con pietoso affetto,
Padre del Cielo, e le sue armate genti
che non ad altro ch'a disfare intenti
son quelli che 'l Tuo nome hanno in dispetto.
E, se lui solo hai fra tant'altri eletto
per dimostrar gli effetti Tuoi potenti,
fa che, confusi li nemici e spenti,
possa render le grazie al Tuo conspetto;
che se con Bursa insieme al gran Romano
desti l'Africa vinta, onde ritenne
de l'Africano poi sempre il cognome,
a questo, che nel mondo unqua non venne
simil a lui, per gloria del Tuo nome
dagli quanto poi dar con larga mano.

Look at the great Charles,[177] Father of Heaven, and his armed troops with caring affection, for those who hold Your name in disdain are wholly intent on our destruction.[178]

Since You have elected[179] him alone among all the others to evince Your powerful actions, make it so that after having dispersed and destroyed the enemies he may present his thanks to You.[180]

If You gave Bursa together with a conquered Africa to that great Roman, who was then known to the world by the name Africanus,[181]

177. Charles V.

178. In reference to the enmity of the Ottoman Empire against the Christian army led by Charles V.

179. The term "eletto" marks Charles V's rule as providentially determined. The poem, like poem 52, identifies Charles V with imperial Rome. Such imagery appears also in Ariosto, *Orlando furioso*, 15.24. For other instances in Gambara's poetry of Charles V as elected by God, see poems 55.5–8 and 57.9–11.

180. Upon Charles V's destruction of Barbarossa's fleet and subsequent capture of Tunis in 1535, the Turkish commander escaped to Algeria to flee Charles V's victorious forces. For further references to Charles V's defeat of Barbarossa, see poems 56.12–14 and 57.12–14.

181. The comparison is between the triumph in Africa of Charles V and that of Cornelius Scipio as told in Petrarch's *Africa*. After his conquest of Carthage in the Second Punic War (202 BCE), Scipio returned to Rome in triumph and was given the territories of Bursa and Africa as well as the surname Africanus.

to this one, who has never had an equal in the whole world, for the glory of Your own name give as much as You can with a generous hand.

55

Quella felice stella e 'n ciel fatale
che fu compagna al nascimento altero
del gran Cesare Augusto, onde l'impero
del mondo tenne, e visse alto e immortale;
quella, ma più benigna, al bel natale
fu guida del gran Carlo, e tal ch'io spero
maggior vederlo, per dir meglio il vero,
e fatto un dio fra noi d'uomo mortale;
che se per vincer gli Indi, e i Medi, e i Sciti,
e i Cantabri, e i Britanni, e i Galli audaci
meritò quel aver tant'alti onori
questo, ch'omai duo mondi ha vinto, e uniti
tanti voler discordi in tante paci,
merita maggior lodi e onor maggiori.

A happy star fated in Heaven accompanied the noble birth of the great Caesar Augustus,[182] after which he held empire over the world and lived high and immortal.

That very one, but even more benevolent, guided the happy birth of noble Charles,[183] so that I hope to see him become even greater, or to better tell the truth, to ascend from mortal man to a god among us.[184]

If for having vanquished the Scythians, Cantabrians, Britons, and the daring Gauls, that one merited so many high honors,[185]

this one, who has already conquered two worlds and united many discordant wills in many truces, merits even greater praise and greater honors.[186]

182. The reference is to Virgil's *Aeneid* 8.881–82, where Augustus is positioned as the glittering star on Aeneas's helmet.

183. Here Gambara likens the birth of Charles V to that of Caesar Augustus, emphasizing the divine benevolence presiding over Charles V's arrival. See notes 167 and 179.

184. A further development of Gambara's conception of Charles V's power. See note 179.

185. In reference to the territories conquered by the Roman Empire under Augustus.

186. The poem places Charles V at the helm of an expanded and unified modern Christian kingdom.

56

Là dove più con le sue lucid'onde
la picciol Mela le campagne infiora
de la mia patria, e che, girando, onora
di verdi erbe e bei fiori ambe le sponde,
al gran nome real, che copre e asconde
le glorie nove e quelle antiche ancora,
farò un tempio d'avorio, e dentro e fora
mille cose vedransi alme e gioconde.
Starà nel mezzo una gran statua d'oro,
e dirà un scritto: «Questo è Carlo Augusto,
maggior di quanti mai ebber tal nome».
D'intorno i vinti regi, e al par di loro
fuggir vedrassi il Turco, empio ed ingiusto,
giungendo a' suoi trionfi altere some.

There, where the delicate river Mella[187] makes the meadows of my homeland blossom with its lucid waters, and in its course decorates both banks with green herbs and beautiful flowers,[188]

I will build an ivory temple to the great royal name[189] that overshadows recent and ancient glories; inside and out one would be able to see thousands of graceful and pleasing scenes.

In the middle there will stand an immense golden statue, and the inscription will read, "This is Charles Augustus,[190] greater than any other who ever bore the name."

187. The river Mella, located in the Gambara family territory outside Brescia. For other poems that reference the river Mella see 32, 33, and 34.

188. This quatrain is redolent of Virgilian bucolic elegy. While in poems 26 and 43, the poet draws on the pastoral landscape as a place to declare the sufferings of love, in this poem the landscape provides the setting for a political monument. Cf. also poem 68.

189. Gambara imagines building a monument in honor of Charles V. For another instance of Gambara's "monumental" poetry, see poem 42, where the poet imagines building a shrine in honor of Vittoria Colonna.

190. The name "Charles Augustus" explicitly links the two emperors Charles V and Caesar Augustus. See note 167.

All around it one will see defeated kings and the impious, unjust Turk in flight, adding heavy burdens to his triumphs.[191]

191. The poem was composed in honor of Charles V's victory over Barbarossa. In this final terzina, Gambara celebrates the end of the hitherto triumphant history of the Turkish Empire, which must now carry the burden of defeat to Charles V. See note 180.

57

Quel che di tutto il bel ricco orïente
e del gran Dario andò superbo e altero
se vincer volse a più d'un rischio fero
se stesso pose, e la sua ardita gente,
e fu più d'una volta anco dolente
quel che soggetto al glorïoso impero
fece 'l Rodano, il Ren, Tamesi, e Ibero,
se ben più d'altri fu saggio e possente.
Ma voi, che 'l Cielo, invitto Carlo, ha tolto
per vero esempio in far palese al mondo
quanto le forze sue sono e son state
con la presenza sola in fuga volto
il gran nemico avete, e posto al fondo
quante glorie fur mai degne e pregiate.

The one[192] who triumphed over the beautiful and opulent Orient and over the great Darius[193] placed himself and his daring men in many harsh dangers in order to achieve victory,

and the one[194] who made the Rhone, the Rhine, and the Thames subject to his glorious empire frequently faced affliction, in spite of the greater power and wisdom he held over most others.

But you, unvanquished Charles,[195] the one Heaven chose as the true example[196] of the eternal force of its powers,

with your presence alone you put the great enemy to flight[197] and exceeded any esteemed and precious glory that ever existed.

192. Alexander the Great.

193. The Persian king Darius was conquered by Alexander the Great at the battle of Issus (333 BCE).

194. Augustus. See notes 167 and 190.

195. Gambara compares Charles V's military prowess to the historic triumphs of Alexander the Great and Augustus to position Charles at the pinnacle of his power.

196. See note 179.

197. The Turkish Barbarossa; see notes 166 and 180.

58

In giovenil etate il mondo vinse
quello di cui il gloriïoso nome
degno tenete, e l'onorate chiome
d'eterna gloria alteramente cinse;
simil desio per far lieta vi spinse
la gran Sposa di Cristo, avendo dome
le genti a lei nemiche e fatto come
fece già mai chi grave incendio estinse.
Così, nel più bel fior degli anni vostri,
col senno e col valor mostrato avete
che 'l secondo Alessandro al primo è uguale.
Stanche dunque saran penne ed inchiostri
anzi che possan dir quel che voi sete;
pur vi faranno eterno ed immortale.

The one whose glorious name you worthily bear[198] conquered the world at a young age and proudly wore the honored crown of eternal glory;

a similar desire inspired you to please the great Bride of Christ,[199] having overcome her enemies, and acted as the one who extinguishes a fierce fire.

Thus, in the splendid prime of your years, with your wisdom and virtue you have revealed to the world that the second Alexander is equal to the first.

Pens and inks will be exhausted before they are able to fully describe your true greatness; even so, they will render you eternal and immortal.

198. In this sonnet, Gambara aligns Alessandro Farnese, Pope Paul III, with the ancient ruler Alexander the Great; cf. poem 57.

199. The metaphor of the church as the bride of Christ originates in Paul's letters to describe the eternal alliance between Christ and his church.

59

Vinca gli sdegni e l'odio vostro antico,
Carlo e Francesco, il nome sacro e santo
di Cristo, e di Sua fe' vi caglia tanto
quanto a voi più d'ogni altro è stato amico.
L'arme vostre a domar l'empio nimico
di lui sian pronte, e non tenete in pianto
non pur l'Italia, ma l'Europa, e quanto
bagna il mar, cinge valle o colle aprico.
Il gran Pastor, a cui le chiavi date
furon del cielo, a voi si volge e prega
che de le greggie sue pietà vi prenda.
Possa più in voi che 'l sdegno la pietate,
coppia real; un sol desio vi accenda:
di vendicar chi Gesù sprezza o nega.

May the holy and sacred name of Christ overcome your outrage and your ancient hatred,[200] Charles[201] and Francis.[202] Care for Christ's faith as much as he has been benign to you—more so than to anyone else.

May your arms stand prepared to repress his impious enemy,[203] and let them not remain in tears—not only Italy, but all of Europe, and wherever is washed by the sea or bordered by a valley or a sun-bathed hill.

The great Shepherd,[204] who was given the keys of Heaven,[205] turns to you and prays that you take pity on his flock.

May pity have more power over you than outrage, royal pair, and may the same sole desire inflame you: to have revenge against those who scorn or deny Jesus.

200. This sonnet is a call for peace between Charles V and King Francis I of France. It was likely composed in the year 1538, when Pope Paul III, the "gran Pastor," summoned the warring kings to partake in peace talks. For other sonnets on the subject, see poem 61.

201. Charles V.

202. Francis I, king of France.

203. The scourge of the Christian empire at this time was the Turkish Barbarossa. See note 166.

204. As throughout Gambara's political poetry, Pope Paul III is referred to as the "pastor santo" who leads the Christian empire. See note 169.

205. See note 208 below.

60

Tu che di Pietro il gloriöso manto
vesti felice e del Celeste Regno
hai le chiavi in governo, onde sei degno
di Dio ministro e Pastor saggio e santo:
mira la greggia a te commessa e quanto
la scema il fiero lupo, e poi sostegno
sicuro l'una dal tuo sacro ingegno
riceva e l'altro giusta pena e pianto!
Scaccia animoso fuor del ricco nido
i nemici di Cristo or che i duo regi
ogni lor cura e studio hanno a te volto!
Se ciò farai non fia men chiaro il grido
de l'opre tue leggiadre e fatti egregi
che fia di quello il cui gran nome hai tolto!

You[206] who happily wear the glorious mantle of Peter and hold the keys to the kingdom of Heaven,[207] making you worthy minister of God and wise, saintly Shepherd:

look at the flock entrusted to you and see how the fiery wolf decimates it.[208] Let that one[209] have steady support from your divine mind, while this one[210] receives well-deserved punishment and pain.

Fiercely expel the enemies of Christ from the rich nest, now that the two kings have turned their every care to you.[211]

206. Alessandro Farnese, Pope Paul III.

207. Gambara refers to the "first pope," Saint Peter, who, according to Matthew 16:19, was given the keys of heaven by Jesus: "I will give you the keys of the kingdom of heaven, and whatever you bind on earth will be bound in heaven, and whatever you loose on earth will be loosed in heaven."

208. The imagery of the saintly pastor alludes to John 10:11–16, in which the good shepherd gathers his sheep scattered by the wolf. See note 169.

209. Referring to "the flock" as the body of Christendom.

210. Referring to "the wolf," the Ottoman Empire, enemy to Christianity.

211. The reference is to the brief peace treaty formed in Nice between Francis I and Charles V in 1538, which the poet hopes will strengthen the force of Christendom against the Ottoman Empire.

If you will do this, the acclamation of your illustrious deeds will be no less resounding than that of the one whose great name you hold.[212]

212. Saint Paul, whose name Alessandro Farnese took as his papal title, Pope Paul III.

61

Ecco che già tre volte, Italia mia,
per sanar le tue piaghe acerbe e gravi
quel ch'in governo ha le celesti chiavi
lieto con Carlo a ragionar s'invia!
Dal gran saper e da la voglia pia
spera aver pace, e i giorni tuoi soavi,
né temer più che ria fortuna aggravi
le belle piagge tue come solia.
Questo è 'l vaso secondo eletto a prova
da Cristo per salvar l'amato gregge,
non men forse del primo e forte e saggio;
questo l'antica gloria in te rinova,
e con la luce del suo santo raggio
rischiara il mondo e gli error suoi corregge.

For the third time, my Italy,[213] to heal your serious wounds, the one who holds the keys to Heaven[214] happily turns to converse with Charles.[215]

Thanks to this one's great wisdom and the other's pious intention, you may now hope for peace and untroubled days, and fear no longer that bitter fortune will cast darkness over your beautiful shores.

He is the second vessel put to the test by Christ to save his holy flock,[216] by no means less strong or wise than the first;

he renews your ancient glory, and with the light of his holy beam, he brightens the world and correct its errors.

213. The opening line evokes the famous political canzone of Petrarch's *Rerum vulgarium fragmenta*, 128.1, "Italia mia" (My Italy).

214. Alessandro Farnese, Pope Paul III. See note 208.

215. This sonnet marks the third congress between Francis I and Charles V to reach a peace treaty in 1543. See also poem 59.

216. The reference underscores Pope Paul III's role as the good shepherd who will save the flock. See note 169.

62

Mira, Signor, la stanca navicella
di Pietro che nel mar da fieri venti
spinta, va errando, e par che si lamenti
di questa fluttüosa e ria procella.
Mira che sola in questa parte e in quella,
smarrita corre, e con dogliosi accenti
Ti dimanda soccorso, e Tu consenti
che finor possa in lei nemica stella?
Nave senza nocchier, senza pastore
non può star gregge, che da l'onde l'una
l'altro è da lupi travagliata e morto;
Signor, dunque, provedi, e il Tuo favore
spira a chi sappia in la maggior fortuna
questa barca condur felice in porto.

Look, Lord, at the weary ship of Peter;[217] tossed about at sea by fierce winds, it wanders and seems to lament this turbulent water and severe storm.

Look at how it carries on, lost and alone, now here now there, and how it cries out for Your help with intense sorrow; and yet You allow an enemy star to have such power over it?

A ship cannot be without a helmsman,[218] nor a flock be without a shepherd,[219] as one would be tormented and finally destroyed by the waves, and the other devoured by wolves.

Hence, Lord, provide for Your vessel, and give Your favor to whoever may be able to steer in the worst of the storm this ship safely into port.

217. The allusion is to the church as a ship lost at sea upon the death of Pope Paul III in 1549. See Dante, *Purgatorio*, 32.127–129.

218. See Dante, *Purgatorio*, 6.76–78.

219. The death of Pope Paul III, the saintly shepherd of the Christian people, has left his flock (the Christian people) without its shepherd. See note 169.

63

La bella Flora, che da voi sol spera,
famosi eroi, e libertate e pace,
fra speranza e timor si strugge e sface,
e spesso dice, or mansueta or fera:
«O de' miei figli saggia e nobil schiera!
Perché di non seguir l'orme vi piace
di chi col ferro e con la mano audace
vi fè al mio scampo aperta strada e vera?
Perché sì tardi al mio soccorso andate?
Già non produssi voi liberi e lieti
perché lassate me serva e dolente!
Quanta sia 'n voi virtù dunque mostrate,
e col consiglio e con la man possente
fate libera me, voi salvi e queti!»

Beautiful Flora,[220] who hopes for liberty and peace only from you, famous heroes, sways between hope and fear, and often says, at times gently, at times fiercely:[221]

"Oh my sons, you wise and noble warriors! Why do you not follow in the footsteps of those who opened for you the path to my salvation with steel and a brave hand?[222]

Why are you so late in coming to my rescue? I did not generate you happy and free for you to let me be enslaved and in distress!

Reveal now how much virtue is in you, and with wisdom and a powerful hand, liberate me, and make yourselves safe and peaceful!"

220. Flora, Roman goddess of flowers, stands here for the city of Florence.

221. Florence is represented as speaking to her (the city's) government.

222. Gambara supported the campaign to dismantle the Florentine Republic orchestrated by Charles V and Clement VII in 1531, and her son very likely served in the imperial army during the campaign. Gambara's letters reveal unwavering support for Medici rule in Florence, thus the sonnet may be read in support of this cause, though we do not have a precise date of composition.

SPIRITUAL POEMS

64

Oh gran misterio, e sol per fede inteso!
Fatto è 'l bel corpo tuo tempio di Dio,
Vergine santa, e 'n quello, umile e pio,
è per propria virtù dal Ciel disceso!
Fu de l'umiltà tua sì forte acceso,
e tanto di salvarne ebbe desio
ch'in te si chiuse, e di te fuori uscio
non tocco il virginal chiostro od offeso!
Creossi in te, come nel bianco vello
la celeste rugiada, arida essendo
la terra ed egli sol d'acqua ripieno!
Questo l'effetto fu, fu il segno quello;
però teco cantiamo oggi dicendo:
«Gloria al Signor, non mai lodato a pieno!»

Oh great mystery, understandable only through faith![223] Your beautiful body, saintly Virgin, was made a temple for God, and in that sacred place, he who is most humble and merciful descended by his own will from Heaven.

He was so enamored of your humility and had such fervent desire for our salvation that he enclosed himself within you and left your virginal cloister without any harm.[224]

He created his self in you, like the heavenly dew in the white fleece; it alone full of water, while the earth remained dry.[225]

This was the effect; that was the sign. Thus, today[226] we sing to you and say, "Glory to God, never fully praised!"

223. A sonnet on Jesus, conceived and born of the Virgin Mary.

224. By tradition, Jesus's birth to Mary was held to have left her body virginal. Luke 1:28–36 tells the story of the Annunciation, where Gabriel tells Mary she will bear God's son.

225. The reference is to Judges 6:36–40, where the dew that forms on the fleece reassures Gideon of God's presence; similarly, Jesus's birth to Mary affirms the grace of God.

226. This sonnet was likely composed to commemorate a liturgical celebration.

65

Oggi per mezzo tuo, Vergine pura,
si mostra in terra sì mirabil cosa
che piena di stupor resta pensosa,
mirando l'opra, e cede la Natura!
Fatto uomo è Dio, e sotto umana cura,
vestito di mortal carne noiosa,
restò qual era, e la divina ascosa
Sua essenza tenne in pueril figura!
Misto non fu, né fu diviso mai,
ma sempre Dio e sempre uomo verace,
quanto possente in Ciel tanto nel mondo!
Volgi dunque ver me, Vergine, i rai
de la tua grazia, e 'l senso mio capace
fa di questo misterio alto e profondo!

Today[227] by means of you, pure Virgin,[228] such a miracle reveals itself on earth that Nature stands in wonder as she marvels at the deed and admits her defeat.

God was made man, and under human care, cloaked in burdensome mortal skin, He remained His true self and hid His divine essence behind the appearance of a human child.[229]

His nature was never mixed, nor ever divided; He remained God and true man at once, as powerful in Heaven as on earth.

Oh Virgin, shine the rays of your heavenly grace on me and help my mortal mind grasp this elevated and profound mystery![230]

227. This sonnet, like poem 64, celebrates a feast day of the church.

228. See Petrarch, *Rerum vulgarium fragmenta* 366.27: "Vergine pura" (Pure Virgin), where he describes the Virgin's body as the vessel for God's manifestation on earth.

229. For the manifestation of God in human form see John 1:14, "And the Word became flesh and dwelt among us, full of grace and truth; we have beheld his glory, glory as of the only Son from the Father."

230. While poem 64 centers on the experience of the Virgin Mary, here the focus is on the presence of God in the body of the child and later, the man. Gambara creates a powerful female construct in positioning the Virgin Mary as the sole figure who understands the mystery.

66

Scelse da tutta la futura gente
gli eletti Suoi l'alta Bontà infinita,
predestinati a la beata vita
per voler sol de la divina mente.
Questi tali poi chiama, e dolcemente
Seco gli unisce ed al ben far gli invita
non per opra di lor saggia o gradita
ma per grazia di Lui, troppo clemente.
Chiamati gli fa giusti, e, giusti poi
gli esalta sì ch'a l'unico Suo Figlio
gli fa conformi e poco men ch'uguali;
qual dunque potrà mai danno o periglio,
ne l'ultimo, di tutti i gravi mali
da Cristo separar i santi Suoi?

The noble and infinite Goodness chose from the future people His blessed elect, predestined to eternal life, solely by the will of His divine mind.[231]

These ones He calls, He gently unites them with Himself, and He prompts them to just actions, not because of any action He found wise or pleasing, but solely by the grace of Him who is most merciful.

With this calling He makes them just, and as such, he exalts them to be little less than equal to His only Son.

Thus, in the moment of the ultimate misery,[232] what harm or danger could ever separate Christ from His saints?[233]

231. Gambara is exploring ideas of predestination. See note 118. Further evidence of Gambara's exploration of predestination can be seen in her eulogy to Bembo upon his death, poem 39.9–11.

232. The "ultimate misery" may refer to death, or to the Day of Judgment.

233. The "saints" (of Christ) refers to the elected.

67

Ne la segreta e più profonda parte
del cor, là dove in schiera armati stanno
i pensier e i desiri, e guerra fanno
sì rea che la ragion spesso si parte,
l'uomo interno ragiona, ed usa ogni arte
per rivocarla e farle noto il danno,
ma dietro a l'altro esterno i sensi vanno
senza al spirito di lor punto far parte.
Di carne sono, e però, infermi e gravi,
capir non ponno i belli alti concetti
che manda il spirto a chi di spirto vive;
guida dunque, Signor, pria che s'aggravi
d'error più l'alma, a le sacrate rive
i miei senza 'l Tuo aiuto iniqui affetti.

In the secret, most hidden region of the heart, where thoughts and desires take up arms and wage war so fierce that Reason often retreats,

the inward man debates and uses every means to call Reason back and reveal the damage caused by her hasty departure, yet the senses follow the outward man, without a word back to the spirit.

They are bound to the material world, weakened and heavy, and thus fail to grasp the elevated concepts the spirit shares with those who live by spirit.[234]

Therefore, Lord, gently guide my innermost feelings, impure without Your help, toward Your sacred shores, lest my spirit further err in its way.

234. This sonnet is rooted in the language and ideas of 2 Corinthians 4:16–18, "Though our outer nature is wasting away, our inner nature is being renewed every day. For this slight momentary affliction is preparing for us an eternal weight of glory beyond all comparison, because we look not to the things that are seen but to the things that are unseen; for the things that are seen are transient, but the things that are unseen are eternal."

STANZE

68[235]

Quando miro la terra, ornata e bella
di mille vaghi ed odorati fiori,
e, come già nel ciel luce ogni stella,
così splendono in lei vari colori,
ed ogni fiera, solitaria e snella,
mossa da natural instinto, fuori
da' boschi uscendo e da l'antiche grotte,
va cercando il compagno e giorno e notte,

e quando miro le vestite piante
di più bei fiori e di novelle fronde,
e che d'augelli le diverse e tante
odo voci cantar, dolci e gioconde,
e, con grato romor, ogni sonante
fiume bagnar le sue fiorite sponde,
talché, di sé invaghita la Natura,
gode in mirar la sua bella fattura,

dico, fra me pensando, «Ahi! Quanto è breve
questa nostra mortal misera vita!
Pur dianzi tutta piena era di neve
questa piaggia, or sì verde e sì fiorita,
e d'un aer turbato, oscuro e greve,
la bellezza del cielo era impedita,
e queste fiere, vaghe ed amorose,
stavan sole, fra monti e boschi ascose;

né s'odivan cantar dolci concenti
per le tenere piante i vaghi augelli,
che dal soffiar di più rabbiosi venti
fatt'eran secche queste e muti quelli,
e si vedean fermati i più correnti
fiumi dal ghiaccio e piccoli ruscelli,
e quanto ora si mostra e bello e allegro
era per la stagion languido ed egro!»

235. Composed in ottava rima.

Così si fugge il tempo, e col fuggire
ne porta gli anni e 'l viver nostro insieme,
ch'a noi, colpa del Ciel, di più fiorire,
come queste faran, manca la speme,
certi non d'altro mai che di morire,
o d'alto sangue nati o di vil seme,
né quanto può donar felice sorte
farà verso di noi pietosa Morte;

anzi, questa crudel ha per usanza
i più famosi e trionfanti regi,
allor ch'hanno di viver più speranza,
privar di vita e degli ornati fregi.
Non lor giova la regia alta possanza,
né gli avuti trofei, né i fatti egregi,
che tutti uguali in suo poter n'andiamo,
né più di ritornar speranza abbiamo.

E pur con tutto ciò, miseri e stolti,
del nostro ben nemici e di noi stessi,
in questo grave error fermi e sepolti
cerchiamo il nostro male e i danni espressi,
e con molte fatiche e affanni molti,
rari avendo i piacer, i dolor spessi,
procacciamo di far noiosa e greve
la vita, che purtroppo è inferma e breve.

Questo, per aver fama, com'accade,
seguendo il periglioso e fiero Marte,
or fra mille saette e mille spade
animoso si caccia, e con questa arte,
mentre spera mostrarsi a le contrade,
ogni gran fatto tenta, ed in disparte
pensa con l'arricchir fars'immortale,
ma casca, poi, sì com'un vetro frale.

Quell'altro, ingordo d'acquistar tesori,
si commette al poter del mare infido,

e di paura pieno, e di dolori,
trapassa or questo ed or quell'altro lido,
e spesso de l'irate onde i romori
lo fan mercè chiamar con alto grido,
e, quando ha d'arricchir più certa speme,
la vita perde, e la speranza insieme.

Altri, ne le gran corti consumando
il più bel fior de' suoi giovenil anni,
mentre ch'util e onor vanno cercando
odio trovano, invidia, oltraggi, e danni,
mercé d'ingrati principi ch'in bando
post'hanno ogni virtute, e sol d'inganni
e di brutta avarizia han pieno il core,
publico danno al mondo e disonore.

Altri, poi, vaghi sol d'esser pregiati
e di tener fra tutti il primo loco,
e per vestirsi d'oro, e andar ornati
de le più ricche gemme, a poco a poco
tiranni de la patria odiosi e ingrati
si fanno, ora col ferro ed or col foco,
ma, alfin, di vita indegni e di memoria,
son morti, e col morir more la gloria.

Quanti son, poi, che divenuti amanti
di duo begli occhi e d'un leggiadro viso
si pascon sol di dolorosi pianti,
da se stessi tenendo il cor diviso!
Né gioia né piacer sono bastanti
trarli dal petto se non finto riso,
e, se lieti talor si mostran fuori,
hanno per un piacer mille dolori!

Chi vive senza mai sentir riposo,
lontano da la dolce amata vista;
chi a se stesso divien grave e noioso
sol per un sguardo o una parola trista;

chi da un novo rival fatto geloso
quasi a par del morir si duol e attrista;
chi si consuma in altre varie pene
più spesse assai che le minute arene.

E così, senza mai stringere il freno
con la ragione a questi van desiri,
dietro al senso correndo il viver pieno
facciamo d'infiniti empi martiri
che tranquillo saria, puro e sereno,
se senza passïon, senza sospiri,
lieti godendo quanto il Ciel ha dato
vivessim in modesto ed umil stato.

Come ne la felice antica etate,
quando di bianco latte e verdi ghiande
si pascevan quell'anime beate,
contente sol di povere vivande,
e non s'odiva fra le genti armate
de le sonore trombe il romor grande,
né per far l'arme li Ciclopi ignudi
battendo risonar facean gli incudi;

né a lor porgeva la speranza ardire
di poter acquistar fama ed onore,
né di perdergli poi grave martire
con dubiosi pensier dava il timore;
né per mutarsi i regni o per desire
di suggiugar gli altrui gioia e dolore
sentivano già mai, sciolti da queste
umane passïon gravi e moleste,

ma senza altri[236] pensier stavan contenti
con l'aratro a voltar la dura terra
ed a mirar i suoi più cari armenti,

236. "Altrui" in Bullock, amended here to "altri" following *Rime*, 1586 ed. See Gambara, *Le rime*, 49.

pascendo insieme, far piacevol guerra;
or con allegri e boscarecci accenti
scacciavano il dolor che spesso atterra
ch'in sé l'accoglie, fra l'erbette e fiori
cantando or con le ninfe or co' pastori.

E spesso a piè d'un olmo o ver d'un pino
era una meta o termine appoggiato,
e chi col dardo al segno più vicino
veloce andava era di fronde ornato;
a Cerere le spiche e a Bacco il vino
offerivan devoti, ed in tal stato
passando i giorni lor serena e chiara
questa vita facean misera e amara.

Questa è la vita che cotanto piacque
al gran padre Saturno, e che seguita
fu dai pastori suoi mentre che giacque
ne le lor menti l'ambizion sopita;
ma come questa poi ria peste nacque
nacque l'invidia, con lei sempre unita,
e misero divenne a un tratto il mondo
prima così felice e sì giocondo.

Perché più dolce assai era fra l'erba
sotto l'ombre dormir, queto e sicuro,
che nei dorati letti e di superba
purpura ornati, e forse più ogni scuro
pensier discaccia, ed ogni doglia acerba,
sentir col cor tranquillo, allegro, e puro
ne l'apparir del sol mugghiar gli armenti
che l'armonia de' più soavi accenti.

Beato dunque, se beato lice
chiamar, mentre che vive, uomo mortale,
e, se vivendo si può dir felice,
parmi esser quel che vive in vita tale;
ma chi esser poi desia qual la fenice,

e cerca di mortal farsi immortale,
ami quella che l'uomo eterno serba,
dolce nel fine e nel principio acerba;

la virtù, dico, che volando al Cielo,
cinta di bella e inestinguibil luce,
se ben vestito è del corporeo velo
con le forti ali sue porta e conduce
chi l'ama e segue, né di morte il zelo
teme già mai, che questo invitto duce,
sprezzando 'l tempo[237] e suoi infiniti danni,
fa viver tal che morto è già mill'anni.

Di così bel desio l'anima accende
questa felice e gloriosa scorta
che a le cose celesti spesso ascende,
e l'intelletto nostro seco porta,
talché del Cielo e di Natura intende
gli alti segreti, onde poi, fatta accorta
quanto ogn'altro piacer men bello sia,
sol segue quella, e tutti gli altri oblia.

Quanti principi grandi amati e cari
insieme con la vita han perso il nome!
Quanti vivono poi gloriosi e chiari
poveri nati sol perché le chiome
di sacri lauri, alteri doni e rari,
s'adornaron felici, ed ora come
chiare stelle fra noi splendon beati!
Mentr'è il mondo staran sempre onorati!

Molti esempi potrei venir contando,
de' quali ne son pien tutte le carte,
che 'l Ciel produtto ha in ogni tempo, ornando,
non sempre avaro, or questa or quella parte,

237. Per Bullock this is "sprezzando i tempo," which is ungrammatical in Italian; amended here to "sprezzando 'l tempo."

ma, quanti ne fur mai dietro lassando
e quanti oggi ne son posti da parte,
un ne dirò che tal fra gli altri luce
qual fra ogn'altro splendor del sol la luce;

dico di voi, o de l'altera pianta
felice ramo del ben nato Lauro,
in cui mirando sol si vede quanta
virtù risplende dal mar Indo al Mauro,
e sotto l'ombra gloriosa e santa
non s'impara aprezar le gemme o l'auro
ma le grandezze ornar con la virtute,
cosa da far tutte le lingue mute.

Dietro a l'orme di voi, dunque, venendo,
ogni basso pensier post'ho in oblio;
seguirò la virtù, chiaro vedendo
esser se non quest'un dolce desio
fallace ogn'altro, e così non temendo
o nemica fortuna o destin rio
starò con questa, ogn'altro ben lassando,
l'anima e lei mentre ch'io viva amando.

When I behold the beautiful land, bountifully adorned with a thousand fragrant flowers, gleaming with various colors just as the stars illuminate the sky, and every wild creature, solitary and swift, moved by a natural instinct, abandoning the ancient caves and woods, roams day and night in search of a companion;

and when I look at the plants embellished with delicate blossoms and freshly budded branches, and hear the multitude of sweet and playful voices of singing birds and the pleasing sound of babbling brooks bathing their blooming banks, so that Nature, filled with pride, delights in contemplating her splendid creation[238]—

238. The opening stanzas depict an elaborate pastoral scene. The trope is present in Gambara's poetry of place as well as in poems 26, 43, and 56.

then I say to myself: "Alas! How brief is this miserable mortal life of ours![239] Not long ago this field, now green and teeming with flowers, was once blanketed with snow; the beauty of the sky was obscured by a dark and stormy wind; and these wild creatures, now so joyful and longing for love, hid isolated and alone in the mountains and woods.

One could not hear the lovely birds singing sweet songs among the tender branches, for the gusts of the most furious winds withered the trees and silenced the birds' song. Cascading rivers and small streams were frozen still by ice, and all that now appears to be full of beauty and joy was made weary and weak by the season."

So time passes by, and in its flight it carries away our years and our lives,[240] since we, bound by the laws of Heaven,[241] lack the hope of ever returning in bloom like these will do. Our only certainty is that we will die, no matter whether of noble or common blood, and whatever gift a blessed fate may bestow upon us, it will never render Death merciful.

On the contrary, this cruel one[242] is known to take away life and signs of glory from the most famous and victorious kings the moment they hold the highest hope in life. Noble and regal powers, conquered prizes won, and exceptional deeds are of no benefit to them, for we all fall equally beneath Death's power, without any hope of return.

Yet still, miserable and, enemies to our well-being and to ourselves, fixed in this grave error, we seek out evident woes and adversities, and with many efforts and great toil, we render a life that is already brief and feeble, burdensome and heavy as well.

239. The phrase recalls Petrarch's canzone 71, "Perché la vita è breve" (Because life is short).

240. See Petrarch's sonnet 361: "'obedir a Natura in tutto è meglio, / ch'a contender con lei 'l tempo ne sforza.' / Subito allor, com'acqua 'l foco amorza, / d'un lungo et grave sonno mi risveglio; / et veggio ben che 'l nostro viver vola / et ch'esser non si po più d'una volta" ('to obey Nature in all is best, for time takes from us the power to oppose her.' Quickly then, as water puts out a fire, I awake from a long and heavy sleep, and I see well that our life flies and that one cannot be alive more than once).

241. In reference to human mortality.

242. In reference to death.

This one, to achieve fame—as happens to those who follow fierce and perilous Mars[243]—boldly throws himself among thousands of arrows and swords, attempting every daring deed, and though within himself he believes this to be the ideal means to gain riches and immortality in fame, he ultimately shatters into a thousand pieces, as fragile as glass.

That other one, greedy for treasures, subjects himself to the power of the treacherous sea. Full of fear and pains, he ventures from shore to shore, the sounds of angry waves often force him to cry aloud for mercy, and just when he nears the highest hope of riches, life and hope vanish at once.

Others waste away the prime of their years in the great courts.[244] While in search of honors, they find instead disdain, envy, contempt, and ruin, all on account of ungrateful princes who have banished every virtue, whose hearts are filled with deceit and hideous avarice, and who are an open disgrace and utter misfortune to the world.

Others who seek solely to be esteemed and to be the first over all others, who dress in gold and go about adorned with the richest gems, little by little, using now iron then fire, become despicable, ungrateful tyrants. In the end they die, unworthy of life and of remembrance, and any glory they had dies along with them.

How many there are, who, after having fallen in love with two beautiful eyes and a lovely face,[245] nourish themselves solely on painful sighs, their heart a stranger to them. No joy or pleasure is ever enough to extract anything but a false smile, and if they ever show the slightest sign of joy, for each pleasure they assuredly feel a thousand pains.

243. Mars, Roman god of war. The reference implies a soldier or general who seeks glory in battle—a quest that ultimately, and inevitably, leads to an untimely downfall.

244. The literary *topos* of the court as a realm of envy and of ruthless competition, where hopes are fostered only to end in ruin and despair, enjoyed great popularity in the Italian Renaissance. Notable examples include Enea Silvio Piccolomini's *De curialium miseriis* (1444), and Pietro Aretino's *Ragionamento delle corti* (1538).

245. The invective against human greed and ambition concludes with a critique of the behavior of one who is swept away by love. The lover's captivation with the "duo begli occhi" is a familiar term in Gambara's oeuvre, a Petrarchan trope that Gambara uses throughout her early love poetry. The *stanze*, first published in 1536, were composed in a later stage of her poetic career, when she no longer wrote sonnets on the theme of love. See note 106.

Some live without rest, far from their sweet beloved face; others become bothersome and annoying to themselves upon the slightest displeasing word or glance; others, made jealous by a new rival, grow sad and ache as if they were about to die; and others consume themselves in pains as various and infinite as grains of sand.

And so, unable to govern these vain desires with reason, we chase after the senses and fill our lives with infinite and impious sufferings—our very lives that could otherwise be tranquil, pure, and serene, if only we lived without passions or sighs in a modest and humble state, happily enjoying the simple gifts bestowed upon us from Heaven.

Such was life in the golden age,[246] when those blessed souls nourished themselves on fresh milk and raw acorns alone,[247] content with meager viands. One heard not the loud noise of trumpets calling men off to war, nor the sound of anvils ringing as the naked Cyclopes[248] hammered out new weapons.

Hope did not give them the boldness to try to gain fame and honor, nor did fear, through doubtful thoughts, give them pain for their loss. Neither the rise and fall of kingdoms, nor the desire to subjugate others, gave them either pain or joy, liberated as they were from these bothersome human passions.

Without any other cares, they were content to plow the land and to watch over their cherished herds as they grazed and playfully skirmished. With joyful, rustic songs, sprawled among the grass and flowers, singing now with nymphs, now with shepherds, they chased away the sorrow that brings down those who allow it into their hearts.

Often a goal or target was leant against the foot of an elm or pine, and the one who arrived closest to the mark with his quick arrow was adorned with the laurel crown. They offered in devotion wheat to Ceres[249] and wine to Bacchus,[250] and passing the days in this state, they made this bitter and unhappy life calm and serene.

246. The *stanze* that follow present an extended meditation on the golden age. Gambara evokes the golden age here, as in poems 31 (a sonnet) and 34 (in ottava rima).

247. See poem 31 for a similar iteration of the pastoral ideal.

248. The Cyclopes forge weapons in Greek and Roman mythology.

249. Ceres is the Roman goddess of agriculture. See also poem 31.

250. Bacchus, the Roman god of wine. See also poem 31.

This was the life that so pleased the great father Saturn,[251] and it was the life pursued by his shepherds, as ambition laid dormant in their minds. But as soon as this bitter plague was born, ambition's eternal companion envy soon followed, and in an instant the world, once so happy and gay, turned to misery.

For it was sweeter to sleep under the shade on the grass, peaceful and safe, than in gilded beds adorned with the richest crimson; and perhaps hearing the lowing of the herds with a tranquil and pure heart at sunrise has more power to dispel every dark thought than the harmony of the most sweet and refined music.

Thus, blessed and happy—if a mortal man can be called such while he is still alive, and if a living man can ever be considered so—seems to be the one who lives such a life. And he who strives to be like the phoenix, who seeks to make himself immortal, should love that which keeps man alive forever, bitter in the beginning, but sweet in the end.[252]

I speak of Virtue, which, flying up to Heaven, emblazoned with beautiful and eternal light, with her strong wings leads and guides whoever loves and follows her,[253] though cloaked in a bodily veil, never fearing the determination of Death, since this unvanquished guide, scorning time and its infinite ruins, keeps alive those who have long been dead.

This happy and glorious guide ignites the soul with such a beautiful desire that the soul often ascends to the celestial realm, carrying with it the intellect, and is thus able to grasp the high secrets of Heaven and Nature together. Then, having realized that every other pleasure is less worthy, the soul follows Virtue alone and forgets all other pleasures.

251. Gambara is evoking the Roman tradition of the golden age, which began when the god Saturn brought agriculture and civilization to the land and, according to Virgil, reigned over a peaceful kingdom. As recounted in *Aeneid* 8, "He [Saturn] made a nation / of those untamed and scattered in high mountains / and gave them laws. And he chose Latium / as name, because he had lain safely hidden / along these coasts. The golden age they tell of / was in the time of this king, for he ruled / his tribe in tranquil peace."

252. The man who strives to be like the phoenix—the mythical bird who dies and rises out of the ashes—seeks immortality in vain.

253. Virtue is the phoenix that rises to the heavens.

Oh, how many prominent and beloved princes lost their fame together with their life! And how many of low birth live glorious and bright only because they happily donned the sacred laurels, superb and unique gifts, and now shine blessed among us like bright stars! They will be honored as long as the world exists!

I could go on counting many examples, already celebrated in all the texts, that Heaven, not always withholding, has produced in every age to honor this or that place. But leaving behind those of times past, and setting aside those who exist now, I will speak of one who shines above all others like sunlight among every other light.

I speak of you, happy branch of the proud plant, the nobly born Laurel.[254] Just looking at you one sees all the virtue that shines from the Indian to the Moorish sea, and under your glorious and saintly shade one learns not how to value gold and jewels, but how to adorn greatness with virtue—something that could silence every tongue.

254. Gambara supported Medici rule of Florence throughout her tenure as the Countess of Correggio. Poem 63, for example, conveys her support of the family in the campaign to dismantle the Florentine Republic orchestrated by Charles V and Clement VII in 1531. While the Duke Cosimo I de' Medici has been identified as the dedicatee of the *stanze*, this cannot be the case as the *stanze* first appeared in print in 1536, and Cosimo did not come into power as duke until 1537 after the unanticipated assassination of his relative Alessandro. The final *stanze* may be read as evoking the golden age of Medici rule under Lorenzo "il Magnifico" de' Medici to convey the promise of Florence's return to grandeur under the family's rule. In this passage, Gambara employs Lorenzo's distinct iconography, with Lorenzo as the virtuous "Laurel" whose evergreen immortality serves as a symbol for the political stability of the city. Verse 4 of Angelo Poliziano's *Stanze per le giostre* provides the model, "Et tu, ben nato Laur, sotto il cui velo / Fiorenza lieta in pace si riposa, / né teme i venti o 'l minacciar del celo / o Giove irato in vista piú crucciosa, / accogli all'ombra del tuo santo stelo / la voce umil, tremante e paurosa; / o causa, o fin di tutte le mie voglie, / che sol vivon d'odor delle tuo foglie" (And you, well-born Laurel, under whose shelter / happy Florence rests in peace, fearing neither / winds nor threats of heaven, nor irate Jove in / his angriest countenance: receive my humble / voice, trembling and fearful, under the shade of / your sacred trunk; o cause, o goal of all my desires, / which draw life only from the fragrance of your leaves). *Stanze*, ed. and trans. David Quint (Amherst, University of Massachusetts Press, 1979). Gambara extends the metaphor of Lorenzo's "nobly born laurel" to praise the virtue of the descendent ("the happy branch") stemming from "the proud plant," rooting Medici family rule in the legacy of Lorenzo de' Medici.

Thus, in following your footsteps, I have consigned every low thought to oblivion.[255] I will follow only Virtue, as I now clearly see that apart from this one sweet desire all others are fallacious. Without fearing a bitter fortune or a cruel destiny, I will stay with Virtue, casting aside every other good, loving my soul and Virtue as long as I live.

255. As in Poliziano's *Stanze* (see note 255), the Medici Laurel inspires the poet to a life of virtue. Gambara employs similar imagery to present herself as a woman of virtue in other poems of this time; see poems 36 and 41; see also note 102.

Bibliography

Editions of Gambara

Gambara, Veronica. *Le rime*. Ed. Alan Bullock. Florence: Olschki; Perth: University of Western Australia Press, 1995.

_____. *Rime e lettere di Veronica Gambara*. Ed. Pia Mestica Chiappetti. Florence: G. Barbèra, 1879.

_____. *Rime e lettere di Veronica Gambara*. Ed. Felice Rizzardi. Brescia: Giammaria Rizzardi, 1759.

Primary Sources

Alighieri, Dante. *La Divina Commedia*. Ed. Anna Maria Chiavacci Leonardi. 3 vols. Milan: Mondadori, 1991–94.

_____. *The Divine Comedy of Dante Alighieri*. Trans. Allen Mandelbaum. 3 vols. Toronto: Bantam Books, 1980–84.

_____. *Monarchia*. Ed. Federico Sanguineti. Milan: Garzanti, 1985.

Amadduzzi, Luigi, ed. *Undici lettere inedite di Veronica Gambara e un'ode latina tradotta in volgare*. Guastella: Tipografia Pecorini, 1889.

Aretino, Pietro. *Edizione nazionale delle opere di Pietro Aretino*. Ed. Giovanni Aquilecchia, Angelo Romano, Danilo Romei. Rome: Salerno, 1992.

Ariosto, Ludovico. *Orlando Furioso*. Milan: Mondadori editore, 1976.

_____. *Orlando Furioso*. Trans. Guido Waldman. Oxford: Oxford University Press, 1974.

Baldacci, Luigi, ed. *Lirici del Cinquecento*. Milan: Longanesi, 1975.

Battiferra degli Ammannati, Laura. *Laura Battiferra and Her Literary Circle: An Anthology*. Ed. and trans. Victoria Kirkham. The Other Voice in Early Modern Europe. Chicago: University of Chicago Press, 2006.

Bembo, Pietro. *Rime*. Ed. Carlo Dionisotti. Turin: Tipografia Icardi, 1971.

_____. *Stanze*. Ed. Alessandro Gnocchi. Florence: Società Editrice Fiorentina, 2003.

Boccaccio, Giovanni. *Famous Women*. Ed. and trans. Virginia Brown. Cambridge, MA: I Tatti Renaissance Library, Harvard University Press, 2001.

Castiglione, Baldassare. *Il libro del cortegiano*. Milan: Garzanti editore, 1981.

Colonna, Vittoria. *Rime*. Ed. Alan Bullock. Rome: Laterza, 1982.

_____. *Sonnets for Michelangelo*. Ed. and trans. Abigail Brundin. The Other Voice in Early Modern Europe. Chicago: University of Chicago Press, 2005.

Correggio, Niccolò da. *Opere*. Ed. Antonia Tissoni Benvenuti. Bari: Laterza, 1969.

Corso, Rinaldo. "Vita di Veronica Gambara" *in Vita di Giberto III da Correggio*. Ancona, 1566. Located in the Biblioteca Nazionale Centrale di Firenze.

Horace. *Odes and Epodes*. Ed. and trans. Niall Rudd. Cambridge, MA: Harvard University Press, 2004.

Medici, Lorenzo de'. *Lorenzo de' Medici Selected Poems and Prose*. Ed. Jon Thiem. Trans. Jon Thiem and Others. University Park: Pennsylvania State University Press, 1991.

The New Oxford Annotated Bible with the Apocrypha, Augmented Third Edition, New Revised Standard Version. Ed. Michael D. Coogan. Oxford: Oxford University Press, 2007.

Nogarola, Isotta. *Complete Writings: Letterbook, Dialogue on Adam and Eve, Orations*. Ed. and trans. Margaret L. King and Diana Robin. The Other Voice in Early Modern Europe. Chicago: University of Chicago Press, 2004.

Petrarch, Francesco. *Petrarch's Africa*. Ed. and trans. T. G. Bergen and A. S. Wilson. New Haven, CT: Yale University Press, 1977.

_____. *Petrarch's Lyric Poems: The "Rime sparse" and Other Lyrics*. Ed. and trans. Robert M. Durling. Cambridge, MA: Harvard University Press, 1976.

_____. *Rime*. Ed. Guido Bezzola. Milan: Rizzoli, 1993.

_____. *Triumphi*. Ed. Marco Ariani. Milan: Mursia, 1988.

Poliziano, Angelo. *Stanze*. Ed. and trans. David Quint. Amherst: University of Massachusetts Press, 1979.

Sappho. *Greek Lyric: Sappho and Alcaeus*. Ed. and trans. David A. Campbell. Cambridge, MA: Harvard University Press, 1982.

Shakespeare, William. *The Complete Sonnets and Poems.* Ed. Colin Burrow. Oxford: Oxford University Press, 2008.

Stampa, Gaspara. *The Complete Poems: The 1554 Edition of the "Rime," a Bilingual Edition.* Ed. Troy Tower and Jane Tylus. Trans. Jane Tylus. The Other Voice in Early Modern Europe. Chicago: University of Chicago Press, 2010.

Tibullus. *Catullus, Tibullus, Pervigilium Veneris.* 2nd ed. revised by G. P. Goold. Cambridge, MA: Harvard University Press, 1988.

Virgil. *Aeneid.* Ed. and trans. Allen Mandelbaum. New York: Bantam Books, 1971.

_____. *Eclogues and Georgics.* Ed. and trans. David R. Slavitt. Baltimore: Johns Hopkins University Press, 1990.

Secondary Sources

Adler, Sara M. "Strong Mothers, Strong Daughters: The Representation of Female Identity in Vittoria Colonna's *Rime* and *Carteggio.*" *Italica* 77 (2000): 311–30.

Ady, Cecilia M. *A History of Milan under the Sforza.* London: Methuen, 1907.

Afribo, Andrea. *Teoria e prassi della "gravitas" nel Cinquecento.* Florence: Franco Cesati, 2001.

Arici, Zelmira. *Bona di Savoia duchessa di Milano (1449–1503).* Turin: Paravia, 1935.

Baernstein, P. Renée. "In Widow's Habit: Women between Convent and Family in Sixteenth-Century Milan." *Sixteenth-Century Journal* 25 (1994): 787–807.

Barolini, Teodolinda. "Dante and Francesca da Rimini: Realpolitik, Romance, Gender." *Speculum* 75, no. 1 (2000): 1–28.

Bassanese, Fiora A. "Private Lives and Public Lies: Texts by Courtesans." *Texas Studies in Literature* 30, no. 3 (1988): 295–319.

_____. "What's in a Name? Self-Naming and Renaissance Women Poets." *Annali d'italianistica* 7 (1989): 104–15.

Bayer, Andrea, ed. *Art and Love in Renaissance Italy.* New York: Metropolitan Museum of Art; New Haven, CT: Yale University Press, 2008.

Bell, Rudolph M. *How to Do It: Guides to Good Living for Renaissance Italians*. Chicago: University of Chicago Press, 1999.

Bennett, Judith M., and Amy M. Froide, eds. *Singlewomen in the European Past, 1250–1800*. Philadelphia: University of Pennsylvania Press, 1999.

Benson, Pamela Joseph. *The Invention of the Renaissance Woman: The Challenge of Female Independence in the Literature and Thought of Italy and England*. University Park: Pennsylvania State University Press, 1992.

Benson, Pamela Joseph, and Victoria Kirkham, eds. *Strong Voices, Weak History: Early Modern Women Writers and Canons in England, France, and Italy*. Ann Arbor: University of Michigan Press, 2005.

Bianco, Monica. "Le due redazioni del commento di Rinaldo Corso alle rime di Vittoria Colonna." *Studi di filologia italiana* 56 (1998): 271–95.

______. "Rinaldo Corso e il 'Canzoniere' di Vittoria Colonna." *Italique, Poésie italienne de la Renaissance* 1 (1998): 35–45.

Bigi, Emilio. *Poesia latina e volgare nel Rinascimento*. Naples: Morano, 1989.

Blade, Melinda K. *Education of Italian Renaissance Women*. Mesquite, TX: Ide House, 1983.

Bloch, Howard. *Medieval Misogyny and the Invention of Western Romantic Love*. Chicago: University of Chicago Press, 1991.

Borgerding, Todd M., ed. *Gender, Sexuality, and Early Music*. New York: Routledge, 2002.

Bowd, Stephen D. *Venice's Most Loyal City: Civic Identity in Renaissance Brescia*. Cambridge, MA: Harvard University Press, 2010.

Bozzetti, Cesare, Pietro Gibellini, and Ennio Sandal, eds. *Veronica Gambara e la poesia del suo tempo nell'Italia settentrionale*. Florence: Olschki, 1989.

Breisach, Ernst. *Caterina Sforza: A Renaissance Virago*. Chicago: University of Chicago Press, 1967.

Broad, Jacqueline, and Karen Green. *A History of Women's Political Thought in Europe, 1400–1700*. Cambridge: Cambridge University Press, 2009.

Brown, Phyllis R., Laurie J. Churchill, and Jane E. Jeffrey, eds. *Women Writing Latin: From Roman Antiquity to Early Modern Europe.* Vol. 3, *Early Modern Women Writing Latin.* New York: Routledge Press, 2002.

Brownlee, Kevin. "Widowhood, Sexuality, and Gender in Christine de Pizan." *Romanic Review* 86, no. 2 (1995): 339–53.

Brundin, Abigail. "Vittoria Colonna and the Virgin Mary." *Modern Language Review* 96 (2001): 61–81.

Bruni, Roberto L., and Diego Zanzani. *Antonio Cornazzanno: La traduzione testuale.* Florence: Olschki, 1992.

Bullock, Alan. "A Hitherto Unexplored Manuscript of 100 Poems by Vittoria Colonna in the Biblioteca Nazionale Centrale, Florence." *Italian Studies* 22 (1966): 42–56.

_____. "Three New Poems by Vittoria Colonna." *Italian Studies* 24 (1969): 44–54.

_____. "Un sonetto inedito di Vittoria Colonna." *Studi e problemi di critica testuale* 2 (1971): 229–35.

_____. "Veronica o Vittoria? Problemi di attribuzione per alcuni sonetti del cinquecento." *Studi e problemi di critica testuale* 6 (1973): 115–31.

Calitti, Floriana. *Fra lirica e narrativa: Storia dell'ottava rima nel Rinascimento.* Florence: Càriti, 2004.

Campbell, Julie. *Literary Circles and Gender in Early Modern Europe.* Aldershot, UK: Ashgate Publishing, 2006.

Carlson, Cindy L., and Angela Jane Weisl, eds. *Constructions of Widowhood and Virginity in the Middle Ages.* New York: St. Martin's Press, 1999.

Carrai, Stefano. *I precetti di Parnaso: Metrica e generi poetici nel Rinascimento italiano.* Rome: Bulzoni, 1991.

Cavallo, Sandra, and Lyndan Warner, eds. *Widowhood in Medieval and Early Modern Europe.* New York: Pearson Education, 1999.

Cerbo, Anna. "Didone in Boccaccio." *Annali Istituto Universitario Orientale, Napoli, Sezione Romanza* 21 (1979): 177–219.

Chabot, Isabelle. "'La sposa in nero': La ritualizzazione del lutto delle vedove fiorentine (secoli XIV–XV)." *Quaderni storici* 86 (1994): 421–62.

_____. "Widowhood and Poverty in Late Medieval Florence." *Continuity and Change* 3 (1988): 291–311.

Chiappetti, Pia Mestica. *Vita di Costanza Varano.* Jesi: Tipografia fratelli Polidori, 1871.

Chiappini, Luciano. *Eleonora d'Aragona: Prima duchessa di Ferrara.* Rovigo: S.T.E.R., 1956.

Chimenti, Antonia. *Veronica Gambara: Gentildonna del rinascimento; Un intreccio di poesia e storia.* Reggio Emilia: Magis Books, 1995.

Chinquini, Chiara. "Rinaldo Corso editore e commentatore delle Rime di Vittoria Colonna." *Aevum* 73 (1999): 669–96.

Chojnacki, Stanley. *Women and Men in Renaissance Venice: Twelve Essays on Patrician Society.* Baltimore: Johns Hopkins University Press, 2000.

Clough, Cecil H. "Daughters and Wives of the Montefeltro: Outstanding Bluestockings of the Quattrocento." *Renaissance Studies* 10, no. 1 (1996): 31–55.

_____. *The Duchy of Urbino in the Renaissance.* London: Variorum Reprints, 1981.

_____. "Federico da Montefeltro and the Kings of Naples: A Study in Fifteenth-Century Survival." *Renaissance Studies* 6, no. 2 (1992): 113–72.

_____. "La successione dei Della Rovere nel Ducato di Urbino." In *I Della Rovere nell'Italia delle corti,* ed. Bonita Cleri, Sabine Eiche, John E. Law, and Feliciano Paoli, 35–62. Urbino: Quattro Venti, 2002.

Clubb, Louise, and William Clubb. "Building a Lyric Canon: Gabriel Giolito and the Rival Anthologists, 1545–1590." *Italica* 68 (1991): 332–44.

Cole, Alison. *Virtue and Magnificence: Art of the Italian Renaissance Courts.* Englewood Cliffs, NJ: Prentice Hall, 1995.

Costa-Zalessow, Natalia. *Scrittrici italiane dal XIII al XX secolo: testi e critica.* Ravenna: Longo, 1982.

Couchman, Jane, and Ann Crabb, eds. *Women's Letters across Europe, 1400–1700.* Aldershot, UK: Ashgate Publishing, 2005.

Cox, Virginia. "The Single Self: Feminist Thought and the Marriage Market in Early Modern Venice." *Renaissance Quarterly* 48, no. 3 (1995): 513–81.

_____. "Sixteenth-Century Women Petrarchists and the Legacy of Laura." *Journal of Medieval and Early Modern Studies* 35, no. 3 (2005): 583–606.

_____. "Women Writers and the Canon in Sixteenth-Century Italy: The Case of Vittoria Colonna." In Benson and Kirkham, *Strong Voices, Weak History*, 14–31.

_____. *Women's Writing in Italy: 1400–1650*. Baltimore: Johns Hopkins University Press, 2008.

Cox-Rearick, Janet. *Bronzino's Chapel of Eleonora in the Palazzo Vecchio*. Berkeley: University of California Press, 1993.

_____. *Dynasty and Destiny in Medici Art*. Princeton, NJ: Princeton University Press, 1984.

de Caprio, Vincenzo. "Dal latino al volgare: Bembo e la ricostituzione della norma." In *Interpreting the Italian Renaissance: Literary Perspectives*, ed. Antonio Toscano, 99–112. Stony Brook, NY: Forum Italicum, 1991.

de Courten, Clementia. *Veronica Gambara: Una gentildonna del Cinquecento*. Milan: Casa Editrice "Est," 1935.

d'Elia, Anthony F. "Marriage, Sexual Pleasure, and Learned Brides in the Wedding Orations of Fifteenth-Century Italy." *Renaissance Quarterly* 55, no. 2 (2002): 379–433.

_____. *The Renaissance of Marriage in Fifteenth-Century Italy*. Cambridge, MA: Harvard University Press, 2004.

Desmond, Marilynn. *Reading Dido*. Minneapolis: University of Minnesota Press, 1994.

de Vries, Joyce. "Casting Her Widowhood: The Contemporary and Posthumous Portraits of Caterina Sforza." In Levy, *Widowhood and Visual Culture in Early Modern Europe*, 77–92.

Dionisotti, Carlo. "Appunti sul Bembo e su Vittoria Colonna." In *Miscellanea Augusto Campana*, ed. Rino Avesani et al., 257–86. Padua: Antenore, 1981.

_____. "Elia Capriolo e Veronica Gambara." In Bozzetti, Gibellini, and Sandal, *Veronica Gambara e la poesia del suo tempo nell'Italia settentrionale*, 13–22.

_____. *Geografia e storia della letteratura italiana.* Turin: Einaudi, 1976.

Dixon, Annette. *Women Who Ruled: Queens, Goddesses, Amazons in Renaissance and Baroque Art.* London: Merrell Publishers, 2002.

Eisler, William. "The Impact of the Emperor Charles V upon the Italian Visual Culture, 1529–1533." *Arte lombarda* 65 (1983): 93–110.

Eisenbichler, Konrad, ed. *The Cultural World of Eleonora di Toledo.* Aldershot, UK: Ashgate Publishing, 2004.

_____. *The Sword and the Pen: Women, Politics, and Poetry in Sixteenth-Century Siena.* Ann Arbor: University of Notre Dame Press, 2012.

Ekserdjian, David. *Correggio.* New Haven, CT: Yale University Press, 1997.

Erickson, Amy Louise. *Women and Property in Early Modern England.* London: Routledge, 1993.

Fantoni, Marcello. "Carlo V e l'immagine dell'*imperator.*" In *Carlo V e l'Italia*, ed. Marcello Fantoni, 77–101. Rome: Bulzoni, 2000.

Felicangeli, B. "Notizie della vita di Elisabetta Malatesta Varano." *Atti della Regia Deputazione di Storia Patria per le provincie delle Marche* 6 (1911): 171–216.

_____. "Notizie sulla vita e sugli scritti di Costanza Varano Sforza, 1426–1447." *Giornale storico della letteratura italiana* 23 (1894): 1–75.

Ferguson, Margaret W. *Dido's Daughters: Literacy, Gender, and Empire in Early Modern England and France.* Chicago: University of Chicago Press, 2003.

Ferrari, Monica. *"Per non manchare in tuto del debito mio": L'educazione dei bambini Sforza nel Quattrocento.* Milan: Franco Angeli, 2000.

ffolliott, Sheila. "Catherine de' Medici as Artemisia: Figuring the Powerful Widow." In *Rewriting the Renaissance: The Discourses of Sexual Difference in Early Modern Europe*, ed. Margaret W. Ferguson, Maureen Quilligan, and Nancy J. Vickers, 227–41. Chicago: University of Chicago Press, 1986.

_____. "The Ideal Queenly Patron of the Renaissance." In *Women and Art in Early Modern Europe*, ed. Cynthia Lawrence, 99–110. University Park: Pennsylvania State University Press, 1997.

Finotti, Fabio. "Women Writers in Renaissance Italy: Courtly Origins of New Literary Canons." In Benson and Kirkham, *Strong Voices, Weak History*, 121–45.

Finzi, Riccardo. *Umanità di Veronica Gambara (1485–1550): Commemorazione pronunciata a Correggio, nel IV centenario della morte della poetessa, il 28 maggio 1950*. Reggio Emilia: Tipolitografia Emiliana, 1969.

Fiore, Silvia R. "The Silent Scholars of Italian Humanism: Feminism in the Renaissance." In *Interpreting the Italian Renaissance: Literary Perspectives*, ed. Antonio Toscano, 15–27. Stony Brook, NY: Forum Italicum, 1991.

Franceschini, Gino. "Battista Montefeltro Malatesta signora di Pesaro." In *Figure del rinascimento urbinate,* ed. Gino Franceschini, 159–65. Urbino: Stabilimento Tipografico Edit. Urbinate, 1959.

Franklin, Margaret. *Boccaccio's Heroines: Power and Virtue in Renaissance Society*. Aldershot, UK: Ashgate Publishing, 2006.

Freedman, Luba. *Titian's Portraits through Aretino's Lens*. University Park: Pennsylvania State University Press, 1995.

Ghidini, Alberto. "La contea di Correggio ai tempi di Veronica Gambara." In Bozzetti, Gibellini, and Sandal, *Veronica Gambara e la poesia del suo tempo nell'Italia settentrionale*, 79–98.

Gilberti, Virginio, Sandro Guerrini, and Dezio Paoletti, eds. *Fasti e splendori dei Gambara: L'apice della potente famiglia bresciana in età rinascimentale e barocca*. Brescia: Associazione Amici Fondazione Civiltà Bresciana della Bassa e del Parco dell'Ogli, 2010.

Giusti, Eugenio L. "The Widow in Giovanni Boccaccio's Works: A Negative *Exemplum* or a Symbol of Positive Praxis?" In *Gendered Contexts: New Perspectives in Italian Cultural Studies*, ed. Laura Benedetti, Julia L. Hairston, and Silvia M. Ross, 39–48. New York: Peter Lang, 1995.

Gold, Barbara K., Paul Allen Miller, and Charles Platter, eds. *Sex and Gender in Medieval and Renaissance Texts: The Latin Tradition*. Albany: State University of New York Press, 1997.

Goody, Jack. *The Development of Marriage and Family in Medieval Europe*. Cambridge: Cambridge University Press, 1983.

Goody, Jack, Joan Thrisk, and E. P. Thompson, eds. *Family and Inheritance in Rural Society in Western Europe, 1200–1800*. Cambridge: Cambridge University Press, 1976.

Gould, Cecil. *The Paintings of Correggio*. London: Faber, 1976.

Greene, Roland. *Post-Petrarchism: Origins and Innovations of the Western Lyric Sequence*. Princeton, NJ: Princeton University Press, 1991.

Greene, Thomas M. *The Light in Troy: Imitation and Discovery in Renaissance Poetry*. New Haven, CT: Yale University Press, 1982.

Griffiths, Gordon, James Hankins, and David Thompson, eds. *The Humanism of Leonardo Bruni*. Binghamton, NY: Medieval and Renaissance Texts and Studies, 1987.

Gundersheimer, Werner L. "Bartolommeo Goggio: A Feminist in Renaissance Ferrara." *Renaissance Quarterly* 33, no. 2 (1980): 175–200.

_____. "Women, Learning, and Power: Eleonora of Aragon and the Court of Ferrara." In Labalme, *Beyond Their Sex*, 43–65. New York: New York University Press, 1980.

Hairston, Julia L. "Skirting the Issue: Machiavelli's Caterina Sforza." *Renaissance Quarterly* 53, no. 3 (2000): 687–712.

Harness, Kelley. *Echoes of Women's Voices: Music, Art, and Female Patronage in Early Modern Florence*. Chicago: University of Chicago Press, 2007.

Haskins, Susan. *Mary Magdalen: Myth and Metaphor*. New York: Harcourt, 1993.

Headley, John M. *The Emperor and His Chancellor: A Study of the Imperial Chancellery under Gattinara*. Cambridge: Cambridge University Press, 1983.

Heiple, Daniel L. *Garcilaso de la Vega and the Italian Renaissance*. University Park: Pennsylvania State University Press, 1994.

Herlihy, David. *Women, Family, and Society in Medieval Europe: Historical Essays (1978–1991)*. Providence: Berghahn Books, 1995.

Hollingsworth, Mary. *Patronage in Renaissance Italy: From 1400 to the Early Sixteenth Century.* London: John Murray, 1994.

Hughes, Diane Owen. "From Brideprice to Dowry in Mediterranean Europe." *Journal of Family History* 3 (1978): 263–96.

Ianziti, Gary. *Humanistic Historiography under the Sforzas: Politics and Propaganda in Fifteenth-Century Milan.* Oxford: Clarendon Press, 1988.

Jardine, Lisa. "'O decus Italiae Virgo,' or the Myth of the Learned Lady in the Renaissance." *Historical Journal* 28, no. 4 (1985): 799–819.

______. "Women and Humanists: An Education for What?" In *Feminism & Renaissance Studies,* ed. Lorna Hutson, 48–81. Oxford: Oxford University Press, 1999.

Jed, Stephanie. *Chaste Thinking: The Rape of Lucretia and the Birth of Humanism.* Bloomington: Indiana University Press, 1987.

Jones, Ann Rosalind. *The Currency of Eros: Women's Love Lyric in Europe, 1540–1620.* Bloomington: Indiana University Press, 1990.

Jones, P. J. *The Malatesta of Rimini and the Papal State: A Political History.* Cambridge: Cambridge University Press, 1974.

Kallendorf, Craig W. "Boccaccio's Dido and the Rhetorical Criticism of Virgil's *Aeneid.*" *Studies in Philology* 82, no. 4 (1985): 401–15.

______. *Humanist Educational Treatises.* Cambridge, MA: Harvard University Press, 2002.

______. *In Praise of Aeneas: Virgil and Epideictic Rhetoric in the Early Italian Renaissance.* Hanover, NH: University Press of New England, 1989.

Kelly, Joan. "Did Women Have a Renaissance?" In *Feminism and Renaissance Studies,* ed. Lorna Hutson, 21–47. Oxford: Oxford University Press, 1999.

Kennedy, William J. *Authorizing Petrarch.* Ithaca, NY: Cornell University Press, 1994.

King, Catherine E. *Renaissance Women Patrons: Wives and Widows in Italy, 1300–1550.* Manchester: Manchester University Press, 1998.

King, Margaret L. "Book-Lined Cells: Women and Humanism in the Early Italian Renaissance." In Labalme, *Beyond Their Sex,* 66–90. New York: New York University Press, 1980.

______. "The Religious Retreat of Isotta Nogarola (1418–1466): Sexism and its Consequences in the Fifteenth Century." *Signs* 3 (1978): 807–22.

______. "Thwarted Ambitions: Six Learned Women of the Italian Renaissance." *Soundings* 59 (1976): 267–304.

______. *Women of the Renaissance.* Chicago: Chicago University Press, 1991.

King, Margaret L., and Albert Rabil Jr., eds. *Her Immaculate Hand: Selected Works by and about Women Humanists of Quattrocento Italy.* Asheville: Pegasus Press, 1997.

Kirkham, Victoria. "Creative Partners: The Marriage of Laura Battiferra and Bartolomeo Ammannati." *Renaissance Quarterly* 55, no. 2 (2002): 498–558.

Klapisch-Zuber, Christiane. *Women, Family, and Ritual in Renaissance Italy.* Chicago: University of Chicago Press, 1985.

Klein, Joan Larson. *Daughters, Wives, and Widows: Writings by Men about Women and Marriage in England.* Urbana: University of Illinois Press, 1992.

Kolsky, Stephen. "Bending the Rules: Marriage in Renaissance Collections of Biographies of Famous Women." In *Marriage in Italy, 1300–1650*, ed. Trevor Dean and K. J. P. Lowe, 227–48. Cambridge: Cambridge University Press, 1998.

______. "Images of Isabella d'Este." *Italian Studies* 39 (1984): 47–62.

Kuehn, Thomas. *Law, Family, and Women: Toward a Legal Anthropology of Renaissance Italy.* Chicago: University of Chicago Press, 1991.

Labalme, Patricia H., ed. *Beyond Their Sex: Learned Women of the European Past.* New York: New York University Press, 1980.

Langdon, Gabrielle. *Medici Women: Portraits of Power, Love, and Betrayal in the Court of Duke Cosimo I.* Toronto: University of Toronto Press, 2006.

Lawless, Catherine. "'A Widow of God?' St. Anne and Representations of Widowhood in Fifteenth-Century Florence." In *Women in Renaissance and Early Modern Europe*, ed. Christine Meek, 15–42. Dublin: Four Courts Press, 2000.

Levy, Alison, ed. *Re-membering Masculinity in Early Modern Florence: Widowed Bodies, Mourning and Portraiture.* Aldershot, UK: Ashgate Publishing, 2006.

_____. *Widowhood and Visual Culture in Early Modern Europe.* Aldershot: Ashgate Publishing, 2003.

Looney, Dennis, and Deanna Shemek, eds. *Phaethon's Children: The Este Court and Its Culture in Early Modern Ferrara.* Tempe: Arizona Center for Medieval and Renaissance Studies, 2005.

Lord, Marie Louise. "Dido as an Example of Chastity: The Influence of Example Literature." *Harvard Library Bulletin* 17 (1969): 216–32.

Lubkin, Gregory. *A Renaissance Court: Milan under Galeazzo Maria Sforza.* Berkeley: University of California Press, 1994.

Lynn, John A. *Women, Armies, and Warfare in Early Modern Europe.* Cambridge: Cambridge University Press, 2008.

Macchia, Giovanni. "Quattro poetesse del Cinquecento." *Rivista rosminiana* 31, no. 20 (1937): 152–57.

Maclean, Ian. *The Renaissance Notion of Woman: A Study in the Fortunes and Scholasticism and Medieval Science in European Intellectual Life.* Cambridge: Cambridge University Press, 1980.

Makowski, Elizabeth M., and Katharina M. Wilson, eds. *Wykked Wyves and the Woes of Marriage.* Albany: New York State University Press, 1990.

Mazzanti, Marinella Bonvini. *Battista Sforza Montefeltro: Una "principessa" nel Rinascimento italiano.* Urbino: Quattro Venti, 1993.

McIver, Katherine A. "The 'Ladies of Correggio': Veronica Gambara and Her Matriarchal Heritage." *Explorations in Renaissance Culture* 26, no. 1 (2000): 25–44.

_____. "Two Emilian Noblewomen and Patronage Networks in the Cinquecento." In Reiss and Wilkins, *Beyond Isabella,* 159–76. Kirksville: Truman State University Press, 2001.

_____. *Women, Art, and Architecture in Northern Italy, 1520–1580.* Aldershot, UK: Ashgate Publishing, 2006.

McLeod, Glenda. *Virtue and Venom: Catalogues of Women from Antiquity to the Renaissance.* Ann Arbor: University of Michigan Press, 1991.

Mirrer, Louise, ed. *Upon My Husband's Death: Widows in the Literature and Histories of Late Medieval Europe.* Ann Arbor: University of Michigan Press, 1992.

Monson, Craig, ed. *The Crannied Wall: Women, Religion, and the Arts in Early Modern Europe.* Ann Arbor: University of Michigan Press, 1992.

Murphy, Caroline. *Lavinia Fontana: A Painter and Her Patrons in Sixteenth-Century Bologna.* New Haven, CT: Yale University Press, 2003.

Och, Marjorie. "Vittoria Colonna and the Commission for a Mary Magdalen by Titian." In Reiss and Wilkins, *Beyond Isabella,* 193–223.

Ong, Walter J. "Latin Language Study as a Renaissance Puberty Rite." *Studies in Philology* 56, no. 2 (1959): 103–24.

Panizza, Letizia, ed. *Women in Italian Renaissance Culture and Society.* London: Legenda Press, 2000.

Panizza, Letizia, and Sharon Wood, eds. *A History of Women's Writing in Italy.* Cambridge: Cambridge University Press, 2000.

Parker, Holt. "Latin and Greek Poetry by Five Renaissance Italian Women Humanists." In Gold, Miller, and Platter, *Sex and Gender in Medieval and Renaissance Texts,* 247–85.

Pittock, Malcolm. "Widow Dido." *Notes and Queries* 33, no. 3 (1986): 368–69.

Poss, Richard. "Veronica Gambara: A Renaissance Gentildonna." In *Women of the Renaissance and Reformation* ed. Katharina M. Wilson, 47–66. Athens: University of Georgia Press, 1987.

Prizer, William F. "Isabella d'Este and Lucrezia Borgia as Patrons of Music: The Frottola at Mantua and Ferrara." *Journal of the American Musicological Society* 38, no. 1 (1985): 1–33.

Pyle, Cynthia M. *Milan and Lombardy in the Renaissance: Essays in Cultural History.* Rome: La Fenice Edizioni, 1997.

Quint, David. "Courtier, Prince, Lady: The Design of the Book of the Courtier." In *The Book of the Courtier,* ed. and trans. Daniel Javitch, 352–65. New York: W. W. Norton, 2002.

Quondam, Amadeo. *Petrarchismo mediato: Per una critica della forma antologia.* Rome: Bulzoni, 1974.

Rabitti, Giovanna. "Vittoria Colonna, Bembo e Firenze: Un caso di recezione e qualche postilla." *Studi e problemi di critica testuale* 44 (1992): 127–55.

Reiss, Sheryl E., and David G. Wilkins, eds. *Beyond Isabella: Secular Women Patrons of Art in Renaissance Italy.* Kirksville, MO: Truman State University Press, 2001.

Rice, Eugene F. *Saint Jerome in the Renaissance.* Baltimore: Johns Hopkins University Press, 1985.

Robathon, Dorothy M. "A Fifteenth-Century Bluestocking." *Medievalia et humanistica* 2 (1944): 106–11.

Robin, Diana. *Publishing Women: Salons, the Presses, and the Counter-Reformation in Sixteenth-Century Italy.* Chicago: University of Chicago Press, 2007.

Rose, Mary Beth. *Gender and Heroism in Early Modern English Literature.* Chicago: University of Chicago Press, 2002.

Rosenthal, Earl S. "Plus Ultra, Non Plus Ultra, and the Columnar Device of Emperor Charles V." *Journal of the Warburg and Courtauld Institutes* 34 (1971): 204–28.

Ross, Sarah. *The Birth of Feminism: Woman as Intellect in Renaissance Italy and England.* Cambridge, MA: Harvard University Press, 2009.

Russell, Rinaldina, ed. *Italian Women Writers: A Bio-Bibliographical Sourcebook.* Westport, CT: Greenwood Press, 1994.

Salamone, Nadia Cannata. "Women and the Making of the Italian Literary Canon." In Panizza, *Women in Italian Renaissance Culture and Society*, 498–512.

Schianchi, Lucia Fomari. *Correggio.* Florence: Scala, 1994.

Shemek, Deanna. *Ladies Errant: Wayward Women and Social Order in Early Modern Italy.* Durham: Duke University Press, 1998.

Smarr, Janet, ed. *Writers Reading Writers: Intertextual Studies in Medieval and Early Modern Literature in Honor of Robert Hollander.* Newark: University of Delaware Press, 2007.

Stevenson, Jane. "Female Authority and Authorization Strategies in Early Modern Europe." In *This Double Voice: Gendered Writing in Early Modern England*, ed. Danielle Clarke and Elizabeth Clarke, 16–40. Basingstoke, UK: Macmillan, 2000.

______. "Women and Classical Education in the Early Modern Period." In Whitehead, *Women's Education in Early Modern Europe*, 83–109. New York: Garland Publications, 1999.

_____. *Women Latin Poets: Language, Gender, and Authority from Antiquity to the Eighteenth Century.* Oxford: Oxford University Press, 2005.

Stroccia, Sharon T. "Remembering Family: Women, Kin, and Commemorative Masses in Renaissance Florence." *Renaissance Quarterly* 42, no. 4 (1989): 635–54.

Strong, Roy. *Art and Power: Renaissance Festivals 1450–1650.* Berkeley: University of California Press, 1984.

Tomas, Natalie. *The Medici Women: Gender and Power in Renaissance Florence.* Aldershot, UK: Ashgate Publishing, 2003.

Trexler, Richard C. *Public Life in Renaissance Florence.* Ithaca, NY: Cornell University Press, 1991.

Vaccaro, Mary. "Dutiful Widows: Female Patronage and Two Marian Altarpieces by Parmigianino." In Reiss and Wilkins, *Beyond Isabella*, 177–92.

Valone, Carolyn. "Piety and Patronage: Women and the Early Jesuits." In *Creative Women in Medieval and Early Modern Italy*, ed. E. Ann Matter and John Coakley, 157–84. Philadelphia: University of Pennsylvania Press, 1994.

_____. "Roman Matrons as Patrons: Various Views of the Cloistered Wall." In Monson, *The Crannied Wall*, 49–72.

van den Bosch, Lourens, and Jan Bremmer, eds. *Between Poverty and the Pyre: Moments in the History of Widowhood.* London: Routledge, 1995.

Vecce, Carlo. "Vittoria Colonna: Il codice epistolare della poesia femminile." *Critica letteraria* 21 (1993): 3–34.

Vela, Claudio. "Poesia in musica: Rime della Gambara e di altri poeti settentrionali in tradizione musicale." In Bozzetti, Gibellini, and Sandal, *Veronica Gambara e la poesia del suo tempo nell'Italia settentrionale*, 399–416.

Welch, Evelyn S. *Art and Authority in Renaissance Milan.* New Haven, CT: Yale University Press, 1995.

Whitehead, Barbara J., ed. *Women's Education in Early Modern Europe: A History, 1500–1800.* New York: Garland Publications, 1999.

Wiesner, Mary E. *Women and Gender in Early Modern Europe.* Cambridge: Cambridge University Press, 1993.

Woodward, William Harrison. *Vittorino da Feltre and Other Humanist Educators*. Cambridge: Cambridge University Press, 1905.

Yates, Frances A. *Astrea: The Imperial Theme in the Sixteenth Century*. London: Routledge, 1975.

Zamboni, Baldassare Camillo. "Vita di Veronica Gambara." In Gambara, *Rime e lettere di Veronica Gambara*, ed. Felice Rizzardi, 25–84.

Index